CORPORATE ETHICS

The Business Code of Conduct for Ethical Employees

By
Steven R. Barth

ASPATORE
C-Level Business Intelligence™

Published by Aspatore, Inc.
For corrections, company/title updates, comments or any other inquiries please email info@aspatore.com.

First Printing, 2003
10 9 8 7 6 5 4 3 2 1

ISBN 1-58762-305-6

Library of Congress Control Number: 2003103749

Cover design by Scott Rattray

Material in this book is for educational purposes only. This book is sold with the understanding that neither any of the authors or the publisher is engaged in rendering medical, legal, accounting, investment, or any other professional service to you directly. For legal advice, please consult your personal lawyer.

This book is printed on acid free paper.

A special thanks to all the individuals that made this book possible.

The views expressed by the individuals in this book (or the individuals on the cover) do not necessarily reflect the views shared by the companies they are employed by (or the companies mentioned in this book). The companies referenced may not be the same company that the individual works for since the publishing of this book.

Publisher of Books, Business Intelligence
Publications & Services

www.Aspatore.com

Aspatore is the world's largest and most exclusive publisher of C-Level executives (CEO, CFO, CTO, CMO, Partner) from the world's most respected companies. Aspatore annually publishes C-Level executives from over half the Global 500, top 250 professional services firms, law firms (MPs/Chairs), and other leading companies of all sizes in books, briefs, reports, articles and other publications. By focusing on publishing only C-Level executives, Aspatore provides professionals of all levels with proven business intelligence from industry insiders, rather than relying on the knowledge of unknown authors and analysts. Aspatore publishes an innovative line of business intelligence resources including Inside the Minds, Executive Edge, Aspatore Business Bibles, Brainstormers, and The C-Level Test in addition to other best selling business books, briefs and essays. Aspatore also provides an array of business services including The C-Level Library, PIA Reports, SmartPacks, and The C-Level Review, as well as outsourced business library and researching capabilities. Aspatore focuses on traditional print publishing and providing business intelligence services, while our portfolio companies, Corporate Publishing Group (B2B writing & editing), Aspatore Speaker's Network, and Aspatore Stores focus on developing areas within the business and publishing worlds.

CORPORATE ETHICS

The Business Code of Conduct for Ethical Employees

1

WHY HAVE
A CORPORATE CODE
OF CONDUCT?

The Importance of a Corporate Code of Conduct

In the wake of the far-reaching financial and societal effects of the dramatic corporate ethical collapses at Enron, WorldCom, Adelphia, Tyco, Arthur Andersen, Waste Management, and others, ethical business conduct has never received so much attention. Because of these and other much publicized corporate ethical meltdowns, Congress, the Securities and Exchange Commission, and our national stock exchanges now require that all publicly traded companies adopt and implement a corporate code of conduct. Prior laws, such as the Foreign Corrupt Practices Act of 1977 and the Federal Sentencing Guidelines of 1991 either require or make it legally beneficial for companies to adopt a corporate code of ethical conduct. Of course, companies in various government-regulated industries, such as banks, broker-dealers, healthcare firms, investment advisors, and investment companies, and those that do business with the federal or state governments, have long been legally required to implement corporate codes of ethical conduct.

But whether your company is publicly held, is a private company, contracts with the government, or is in a government-regulated industry, establishing, communicating, and enforcing a comprehensive set of ethical rules of business conduct for your organization can provide tremendous tangible business and legal benefits.

Ethics play a central role in many of the daily decisions your company's employees make. With the increasing diversity and multi-cultural backgrounds of our country's employee base, employees have widely different personal and cultural perceptions of what type of conduct is acceptable and what is unethical. It's not always easy for employees to decide whether an issue raises legal or ethical concerns and, if it does, then to determine "the right thing to do," particularly from your company's perspective. Since this trend will only continue, educating your employees on proper business conduct and ethics and implementing a unified corporate code of conduct for your workforce are more important than ever.

Adopting a set of well-understood and enforced companywide business conduct rules will help educate your employees so they can recognize and identify legal and ethical issues when they first arise. If your employees can't identify situations that raise legal or ethical concerns, it's highly unlikely they'll handle the situations properly, particularly from your company's point of view.

7

A corporate code of conduct can set forth important ground rules that will enable your employees to react to legal and ethical dilemmas responsibly and consistently throughout your organization. A corporate ethics code can establish fundamental decision-making rules, guidelines, and procedures your employees can apply like a roadmap in dealing with the legal, ethical, and moral dilemmas they face daily in conducting your business. As Supreme Court Justice Stewart Potter said when defining ethical conduct, "It is one thing to know what you have a right to do, but it's even more important to know what is the right thing to do." A good corporate ethics code, properly implemented, will help your employees make these right decisions.

Your corporate code of conduct can incorporate your fundamental philosophies on how your company wants to do business and be known by those with whom your company does business. A code of conduct can set forth your company's vision, mission, and guiding business principles, which will help set the overall tone and basis for your employees to apply your code to individual circumstances.

A corporate code of conduct can help establish a moral and ethical compass for your workforce, pointing your employees toward the "true north" for commitment to business practices that are fair, civil, and respectful. By instilling these cultural values throughout your organization, you can then create the baseline for establishing personal employee responsibility and accountability in meeting well understood organizational standards of ethical and moral conduct.

Adopting a corporate code of ethical business conduct will enable your company to create a cohesive culture of doing the right thing for the right reasons. A corporate culture that embraces this credo and emphasizes that your company will not conduct business in any other manner will not only help prevent your company and your employees from violating the law, but it will also help limit your company's liability exposure should an ethical or legal lapse subsequently occur.

Perhaps even more importantly, implementing and enforcing an effective corporate code of ethical business conduct will help improve your employees' self-esteem and morale, making them happier and more productive.

A corporate code can enhance your company's business reputation and image in the eyes of your customers, your suppliers, and the communities in which you operate. As a result, your code of conduct can lead to more and better business for your company – business with fewer risks of recrimination or liability.

In his article "Do It Right" in the November 2001 issue of the *MBA Jungle,* author Jeffrey Seglin demonstrated that practicing ethical business usually has a positive impact on a company's bottom line. Seglin cited a 1992 study published by Harvard Business School professors John Kotter and James Heskett in which 207 large U.S. firms were studied over a period of 11 years. When comparing firms having an emphasis on business ethics to those with a narrow focus on profits, Kotter and Heskett discovered greater increases in revenue (682 percent vs. 166 percent), workforce (282 percent vs. 36 percent), stock price (901 percent vs. 74 percent), and net income (756 percent vs. 1 percent) among the firms with an ethics focus.

In the same article, Seglin cited KPMG Consulting's 2000 Organizational Integrity Study to show that companies whose management is perceived to be ethical by customers and employees often have a better bottom line. Of 2,390 workers surveyed, 69 percent believed their current customers would recommend their company to others. Inherent in that figure, 80 percent of workers who believed their firm's management upheld their company's ethical standards thought customers would recommend their company. But only 40 percent of workers who believed their company's management ignored unethical behavior thought customers would recommend their company. Similarly, 66 percent of all workers surveyed said they would recommend their company to potential new employees. Breaking down that statistic, 81 percent of workers who believed management to be ethical would recommend their own company, while only 21 percent of workers who believed management to be unethical would recommend their own company. Seglin concluded that ethical companies can enjoy increased profits from customer referrals and decreased recruiting costs from employee referrals.

Adopting a corporate code of conduct makes it clear to your employees and to those with whom your company does business the level of seriousness with which your company takes its commitment to ethical business conduct. A code announces to the world that ethics matter at your company by creating well understood expectations of appropriate and inappropriate employee behavior. The educational process alone of adopting and implementing a code of acceptable business conduct will raise the level of ethical consciousness within your company so that legal and ethical problems can be more easily identified and handled properly.

It may not be true that a good corporate code of conduct will result in the actual practice of good business ethics by your company's employees. But, it will certainly be much more difficult to achieve companywide standards of excellent business ethical practices without having a written code of conduct.

Implementation Is Critical

While many companies already have ethics codes in place, few positively affect employee behavior because they have not been properly adopted, implemented, or enforced. Simply having a written code of conduct is not enough to do much good. It takes a real, ongoing organizational commitment to emphasize the critical importance of ethical business conduct, starting at the top of your company, to achieve effective results and tangible business and legal benefits from a corporate code. This commitment must be not only highly evident during the rollout phase of your corporate code, but it must also be ongoing and proactive.

Corporate Culture and Values

A corporate code of conduct should reflect and articulate your company's "personality" – your company's corporate culture and organizational values, ideals, and business philosophies. For example, according to the Business for Social Responsibility, SmithKline Beecham used the development of its code in 1998 as a way to articulate the five core values that define its culture: customers, innovation, integrity, people, and performance.

Similarly, BellSouth's Code of Conduct starts by stating BellSouth's core values:

Our Customers: We are driven by the needs of our customers. We understand our customers' needs and deliver innovative products and services to meet those needs.

Our People: We respect each other. We work together as one BellSouth team. This team reflects the diversity of the communities we serve.

Our Community: Everywhere we do business we strive to make our communities better places to live, work and grow.

Excellence: We strive for excellence in everything that we do, including excellent service for our customers, a great place to work for our employees and outstanding earnings for our shareholders.

Integrity: Every action we take reflects the highest ethical standards. We interact with our customers, our employees and our shareholders with honesty and integrity.

Codes play a critically important part in creating an internal cohesive culture of compliance and of "doing the right thing." For example, Superior Services, Inc. (n/k/a Onyx Waste Services, Inc.), a Milwaukee-based company that collects, transports, and disposes of solid waste in 17 or more states across the country, combines its written corporate code of conduct with its corporate name to firmly establish, within and outside the company, that all of its employees are expected to always act so their organization will be known by all, internally and externally, as a "superior" company. Superior's code of conduct, together with a rigorous employee ethical training program, has firmly established a well understood companywide standard of always "doing the right thing." Compliance with the law and with the moral values of trust and fair play are non-negotiable at Superior.

As a result of this emphasis, acting in a "superior" manner has become infectious throughout Superior's entire organization, from the company's chief executive officer, who has always strongly set the right ethical tone, all the way down to the drivers of its garbage trucks. This organizational attitude and emphasis on "doing the right thing" has been reflected in the increased high quality of the work and customer service of Superior's employees. Customers have recognized a competitive difference, as have Superior's communities and other constituencies, and it has paid off in more business and avoiding breaches of its customers' and the public's trust. Superior's "superior" culture was also one of the reasons the French conglomerate, Vivendi SA, purchased Superior for a premium price in June 1999.

Image and Reputation

For many businesses, their public image and reputation are the core of their values, both financially and psychologically. No one wants to do business with a company that lies, cheats, and swindles. They want to do business with people and companies they think are fair and reasonable and that they can trust. For example, Dow Chemical's Code of Business Conduct states, "our most valuable asset is our outstanding reputation, and it is up to all of us to protect it."

A corporate code of conduct can be a critical element in developing your company's corporate image and reputation and establishing the trust of those with whom your company does business. A corporate code can have an important impact on your company's relationships with its investors, lenders, customers, vendors, and employees, as well as with the cities and towns in which your company operates.

Additionally, in this post-Enron era, stock market investors and business acquirers are increasingly willing to pay a premium value for a company with a management team and employee base that is well grounded on strong ethical and moral values. A 2002 McKinsey Investor Survey found that 63 percent of investment fund managers avoid poorly governed companies, and 57 percent of fund managers indicated they would buy or sell a company's stock based on their corporate governance practices. With the increased public scrutiny and government regulation of corporate governance and business ethics, this trend will continue.

Morale

A corporate code of conduct can be instrumental in improving your companywide morale by encouraging employee teamwork and collegiality and by establishing and benchmarking organizational loyalty and trustworthiness. Like your customers and suppliers, your employees also want to work for a company that will treat them fairly and honestly. They want to work for an organization that will listen to and respect their opinions, even if – and particularly if – their views are different from management's.

A corporate code can help sensitize your management and employees to others so that they will better accept, tolerate, and respect honest differences of opinion. This attitude fosters the resolution of business issues through openness and honesty and by applying shared values of fairness, respect, and responsibility. This approach helps create a healthy workplace environment that will enhance the skills development of your employees and create a positive, empowering workplace atmosphere where your employees believe they truly matter. It will also help improve how your management and employees treat your fellow employees, customers, and suppliers. The result of this positive workplace environment will be increased employee enthusiasm, productivity, and retention. Once word gets out that your company treats its employees with respect and honesty, your ability to attract and retain high-caliber employees will be greatly enhanced.

Discouraging Deception and Dishonesty

A corporate code will not only provide guidance and direction to help your employees avoid violating the law and engaging in unethical behavior, but it will also help your employees avoid engaging in more general acts of unethical and immoral conduct – acts involving deception, dishonesty, cheating, and taking shortcuts, for instance. Adopting and implementing a code of conduct will help your company discourage your employees from engaging in activities for purely personal self-gain that could hurt the best interests of your company and your stockholders.

Opening Communication Channels

A corporate code can help your company open communication channels among your line employees, their supervisors, and higher management to help them report and protect your company against illegal or unethical activities within it. Contrary to the warnings of some critics that this reporting process creates a "snitch" mentality reminiscent of George Orwell's *1984,* most believe that creating and encouraging code violation reporting obligations creates a healthful, self-regulatory environment of checks and balances.

Avoiding Legal Liability and Prosecution

A corporate code of conduct can be instrumental as a risk management tool to help prevent your company and your employees from violating the law and engaging in behavior that otherwise might result in legal prosecution, litigation, or fines against your company, board of directors, management, and employees. The adage about an ounce of prevention being better than a pound of cure has never been more applicable than in preventing litigation. If your company actively and effectively attempts to self-govern its employees' behavior, you stand a much better chance of avoiding attempts by the government or some other entity to govern or regulate the behavior of your company or your employees for you.

Your company's code of conduct should insist that your employees conduct your company's business in full compliance with applicable laws, regulations, and rules. An employee's failure to do so should be a clear violation of your company's code of conduct, since it can expose not only your employee, but also your company and your management, to criminal or civil prosecution, fine, or penalty.

If your company has an effective corporate code of conduct, it can be used as a defense to minimize your company's liability if an employee violates the law or takes an action that results in prosecution or litigation against your company. Implementing an effective code, along with other legal and ethics compliance procedures, can also help your company's board of directors and management defend against potential personal liability for the actions of their subordinates.

Under the Federal Sentencing Guidelines, sanctions, fines, and penalties that might otherwise be imposed on your company for illegal activity by your employees can be greatly reduced, or even avoided altogether, if your company can show that it has in place an effective corporate conduct compliance program. These Guidelines state specifically that, to minimize your company's potential legal liability for an employee's ethical or legal lapse, your company "must have established compliance standards and procedures to be followed by your employees that are reasonably capable of reducing the prospect of criminal conduct."

To obtain the legal benefits of the Federal Sentencing Guidelines, your company must both adopt a written code of conduct and implement it actively and effectively. Under the Guidelines are seven requirements for an effective ethical compliance program. One of these requirements is that "the organization must have taken steps to communicate effectively its standards and procedures to all employees, e.g., by requiring participation in training programs or by disseminating publications that explain in a practical manner what is required."

A written code of conduct, without an active and effective implementation program, won't be worth the paper it is written on in helping your company avoid legal liability or prosecution under the Federal Sentencing Guidelines. In fact, having a written code in place that is not implemented and enforced may be even more damaging, legally, to your company.

But your company shouldn't adopt and implement a code of conduct solely because you are motivated to limit your company's legal liability resulting from the future potential illegal or unethical activities of your employees. Your company should adopt and effectively implement a code of conduct to prevent your employees' illegal or unethical activities from occurring in the first place.

Managing Public Reaction to Ethical Lapses

A code of conduct, properly adopted, implemented, and enforced, can greatly enhance your company's ability to weather a storm of public criticism if a legal or ethical lapse should occur in your company. In such instances, you can show the media and the public that your company has long had in place, and enforced, a code of ethical conduct that prohibits illegal and unethical behavior by your employees and that your company has always exhibited a good faith commitment to preventing such types of unacceptable behavior. As a result, you should be able to convincingly explain to the media and the public that any such unethical or illegal behavior is an isolated, aberrational instance that will not be repeated.

Treating Your Customers Ethically

Another benefit to your company of adopting and implementing a corporate code of conduct is the establishment of policies and procedures on how your company's employees should treat your customers and how your company's products and services should be marketed and sold. One of your company's primary goals that can be highlighted in your corporate code is for your employees to deal with your customers lawfully, ethically, and fairly at all times, regardless of their relative size or importance. Your company's code of conduct can and should emphasize to your employees that your company is committed to providing high-quality services and products to your customers at fair prices and in honest transactions.

Your corporate code can and should make it clear to your employees that they should not "buy business" from your customers. Your code should restrict your employees from providing cash, material gifts, trips, loans, or favors to your customers in an attempt to unduly influence their decision to buy your products or services. This policy will help stress to your company's employees that your products and services need to be sold based on their competitive merits and not through other means.

Your code can also stress that your employees should never engage in any misrepresentation, fraud, or omission of information to your customers.

This subject is discussed in more detail in Chapter 4.

Treating Your Suppliers Ethically

Your company can use a code of conduct to establish policies and procedures on how your employees should treat your company's suppliers and vendors and how your company should purchase products and services from your suppliers and vendors. Your code should emphasize your commitment to engaging in fair competition, without discrimination or deception, in a manner that creates long-lasting business relationships with your suppliers.

Your company's code can and should stress that your employees should deal with all of your company' vendors and suppliers impartially, fairly, honestly, and openly, regardless of their relative size or importance to your company.

Your code can also be used to emphasize to your employees that they are prohibited from taking any action that would unduly influence or restrict your company's purchasing decisions. Procurement decisions by your company should be made solely on the basis of quality, service, price, delivery, best value, or other similar competitive factors. Your code can explain to your employees that they should avoid actual and perceived conflicts of interest and the appearance of partiality or preferential treatment in business transactions with your suppliers and vendors.

This subject is discussed in more detail in Chapter 5.

Treating Your Company Ethically

Your company's corporate code of conduct can and should be used to make it clear to your employees that they owe a duty of loyalty to your company. This will allow your company's employees to understand that your company's business interests must be placed above their own personal self-interests when dealing with issues, transactions, and opportunities that may present an actual or perceived conflict of interest between your employees and your company or that present a "corporate opportunity" for your company.

Your company's code can also require the devotion of your employees' business time and attention to your company. While your employees' rights to engage in private activities should always be respected, your code of conduct can prohibit or strictly limit their ability to moonlight on a second job or engage in other outside-of-work activities or organizations that would affect the performance of their job at your company or that would otherwise embarrass or disadvantage your company.

Your company's code of conduct can be used to reinforce your employees' obligations to safeguard the confidentiality of your company's proprietary and sensitive business information, processes, practices, and trade secrets, and refrain from the disclosure or improper use of any proprietary or sensitive business information, processes, practices, or trade secrets of your company's customers or suppliers, as well as your company's competitors. Your code can also make it clear that new employees should not use confidential information from their previous employers in their jobs with your company.

This subject is discussed in more detail in Chapter 6.

Treating Your Competition Ethically

Your corporate code can make it clear to your employees that your company is committed to competing vigorously for business, in a fair and honest manner, based solely on the competitive merits of your company's products and services. Your code can and should prohibit your employees from taking actions that limit competition with your company or that would violate the antitrust laws. Your code can and should prohibit your employees from colluding or working together with your company's competitors to make agreements on pricing, rates, trade practices, costs, territories, or customers.

Similarly, your code of conduct can and should prohibit your employees from spreading disparaging rumors or malicious gossip about any of the products, services, or employees of any of your company's competitors.

This subject is discussed in more detail in Chapters 7 and 11.

Treating Your Employees Ethically

Another principal benefit to your company of adopting a code of conduct is to express your organizational commitment to treating your employees fairly and equally in all situations and to maintaining employment practices based on equal opportunity. Your code can communicate your organizational respect for your employees' privacy and the treatment of all of your employees with dignity, regardless of their race, color, religion, sex, national origin, age, veteran status, or disability. Your code can reflect your company's commitment to providing safe and healthy working conditions and an atmosphere of open communication for all your employees.

Your company's code of conduct can and should also expressly prohibit harassment or discrimination of any kind against any of your employees.

This subject is discussed in more detail in Chapter 8.

Treating Your Community Ethically

Emphasizing your company's commitment to being a responsible corporate citizen of the communities in which your business operates is another way your company's code of conduct can set precedential values for your employees. Your code can stress your company's commitment to making the cities and towns where your company operates better places to live. Your code can effectively communicate and reinforce your corporate commitment to abiding by all national and local laws and your company's focus on improving the well-being of the communities where your company operates through the encouragement of employee participation in civic affairs and corporate philanthropy.

Similarly, your company's code of conduct can encourage the protection of the environment as part of your organizational philosophy of business conduct. Your code can also ensure that your employees understand they have the responsibility to make certain your products and operations meet applicable government and company standards. Additionally, your code can promote the elimination of all workplace injuries, the prevention of adverse environmental and health impacts, the reduction of wastes and emissions, and the promotion of resource conservation at every stage of the life cycle of your products.

This subject is discussed in more detail in Chapter 9.

Properly Handling Conflicts of Interest

One of the most common types of ethical concerns faced by companies is conflict of interest situations. Your company should generally allow your employees to be free to make personal investments and enjoy social relations and normal business courtesies. But, one of the key benefits to your company of adopting a corporate code of conduct is to better educate your employees on what situations create an actual or perceived conflict of interest and how to avoid them.

Your company's code of conduct can and should make it clear that your employees should not have any personal interests that conflict with the business interests of your company, or that might influence or appear to influence or interfere with their exercise of objective judgment in performing their work-related duties and responsibilities.

A conflict of interest occurs when your employee permits the prospect of his or her direct or indirect personal benefit or gain to improperly influence his or her judgment or actions in the course of doing his or her job for your company. A conflict of interest can arise, for example, where your employee has a personal financial interest that could affect his judgment; gains personal enrichment through access to confidential information; or misuses his position at your company in a way that results in personal gain. A conflict of interest can also arise when your employee has a personal interest, direct or indirect, in a supplier or customer. An indirect interest would arise if an immediate family member of an employee has an interest in a supplier or customer.

Your code of conduct can also communicate to your employees that certain activities could present an actual or perceived conflict of interest and should therefore be avoided.

This subject is discussed in more detail in Chapter 6.

Technological Ethical Dilemmas

In our increasingly high-tech age, a corporate code can help your company educate your employees on how they should appropriately use their company-provided computers, emails, voicemails, facsimile machines, and Internet access.

This subject is discussed in more detail in Chapter 6.

International Business Benefits

As we deal more and more in a global economy, a corporate code of ethical business conduct can greatly benefit your company in your relationships with customers, suppliers, and governments in other countries. Despite vastly different cultures, laws, governments, mores, and conventions, establishing international corporate core fundamental values of fair play and honesty can go a long way toward overcoming foreigners' fear of doing business with your company.

Similarly, your company's code of conduct can help unite your company's diverse global operations. No matter where your offices and employees are located, your code of conduct will help guide your employees to apply cohesive and standardized rules of conduct that promote and are consistent with your company's fundamental business philosophies and values.

This subject is discussed in more detail in Chapter 14.

2

IMPLEMENTING YOUR CORPORATE CODE OF CONDUCT

Effective adoption and implementation of your company's corporate code of conduct is critical to positively affecting the day-to-day legal and ethical behavior of your company's employees. Unfortunately, many companies adopt a written code of corporate conduct that only collects dust on their human resource manager's bookshelf. In these instances, more often than not, the company's code seems to be taken from the shelf, dusted off, and read only when the company is trying to react to an employee's inevitable lapse of legal or ethical conduct. Obviously, this is not an effective way to have a positive impact on the behavior of your company's employees and prevent legal and ethical violations from occurring in the first place.

Setting the Tone at the Top

An effective corporate code of conduct must first be implemented at the top of your organization. According to the 1999 Conference Board Report on Ethical Conduct, more than 95 percent of CEOs are involved in developing their company's code of ethics.

Your company's board of directors and CEO must make a specific, well publicized commitment to adopting and implementing a corporate ethical code and to communicating strongly its fundamental principles and importance throughout your organization. If your company is closely held, this commitment should come from your company's owners, as well. If your company's most senior executive doesn't set the tone at the top, it is unlikely your line employees will place much importance on ethical business conduct. If ethical conduct doesn't seem important to the boss, it won't be important to your company's rank and file employees.

Establish Fundamental Business Principles

The next step in implementing your company's code of conduct should be developing its fundamental business principles and philosophies. This should be done by the board of directors, the CEO, and other key management team members. Your initial code of conduct drafting team should include your chief financial officer, general counsel, human resources manager, vice presidents of sales and procurement, and other critical department officers and managers. If your company is closely held, your owners should be involved in this step. It will also help to have your public relations expert attend these development sessions to ensure your code is clearly written and easily understood from the outset.

Sometimes, as part of this development process, companies survey their employees, or a core group of employees, to solicit their views on how the company should do business and be perceived by others. This process can be very effective in creating early employee awareness of your company's emphasis on ethical conduct, as well as early employee buy-in to the fundamental goals and objectives of your code.

After this process is complete, you should be able to draft a code of conduct that sets forth your management team's view of your company's fundamental business values and guiding ethical principles and philosophies on how your company wants to conduct its business and be perceived by its core constituencies.

Addressing Specific Situations

Next, your management team, led by your general or outside legal counsel, should address in your company's code of conduct the various laws, regulations, rules, and specific areas of potential legal liability that are most likely to apply to your company and its employees. Special attention should be given to the areas in which your company, board of directors, and managers may be most subject to vicarious liability as a result of potential illegal or unethical activities undertaken by your employees.

Your draft code should also address how you want your employees to treat each of your company's key constituencies – your customers, suppliers, shareholders, and communities. It should also set forth how you would like your employees to react to various types of ethical situations with which they are typically faced in the ordinary course of business.

Achieving Broad-Based Employee "Buy-In"

After your board of directors and CEO (and business owners, if your company is closely held) have made clear throughout your organization the importance of your company's organizational commitment to legal and ethical business behavior, and your management team has drafted a corporate code of conduct that incorporates your company's core ethical business conduct principles and specific applications, then you should obtain broad-based, bottoms-up "buy-in" from the employees.

To be most effective, your corporate code should not simply be a commandment that comes down from Mt. Olympus; instead, developing your company's code of conduct, including your core principles and philosophies and specific applications, should involve the input and suggestions of your employees. This open, transparent, and high-profile organizational input process will help your code be understood, embraced, and effective throughout your company. A broad-based code development process, by itself, can also have a dramatic positive impact on your employees' legal and ethical behavior even before your code is completed. Often the process your company undertakes to develop and implement your code is as important as, if not more important than, your resulting written corporate code of conduct.

Your company should try to involve small but diverse employee focus groups from different departments and office locations in reviewing and commenting on the initial draft. These groups should be asked to address what your code should promote and what it should prevent. Then, your draft code should be analyzed by your employees against their expectations and required activities. This takes time and effort, but it is the best way to effect a true organizational consciousness of, and commitment to, corporate ethics.

After your employee focus groups have met and you've begun to add some more substantive content into your draft code, you should next hold some larger employee meetings to discuss the ethical principles underlying your corporate code. Your employees should be asked for suggestions, based on their experiences, on how best to tailor your company's broad ethical principles to apply to specific ethical and moral dilemmas and situations that typically occur at your company. These meetings should involve employees at *all* levels and in *all* departments. Make sure to involve your employees from different geographic locations, particularly from your international operations, to ensure your code incorporates diverse cultural and geographic perspectives and is fully understood and embraced throughout your organization. These larger group discussions can be very effective in bringing your corporate code of conduct to life in the minds of your employees.

This bottoms-up development process should generate several drafts of your company's corporate code, with much discussion and analysis at all levels. This process can result in great benefits to your company. The more your employees are aware of your company's core ethical values, think and talk about legal and ethical behavior, and understand how they should react to specific legal and ethical dilemmas, the more positive impact the process itself will have on how your employees conduct your company's business.

Involving Outside Key Constituencies

Many companies successfully involve their key customers, suppliers, and communities in developing their corporate code of conduct, with several important benefits.

First, your best customers, suppliers, and communities are alerted to your company's true organizational commitment to ethical business conduct. This should help provide tangible business benefits, not only from their better understanding and appreciating your company's commitment to ethical behavior, but in also being honored by being asked to help you develop rules and procedures to ensure that they will be treated fairly and honestly by your company.

Second, this outreach process and understanding of your code should help your customers and suppliers avoid tempting your employees to violate your company's code.

Third, your corporate code will be better coordinated with the ethical rules and procedures of your customers and suppliers. Since it often takes two parties to create an unethical or illegal situation, this should enhance your company's and your constituencies' ability to prevent the occurrence of unethical or illegal behavior.

Finally, this process should help you expand the specific types of ethical situational issues addressed by your code so it can better anticipate potential ethical issues.

Types of Codes of Conduct

There is no formulaic, one-size-fits-all type of corporate code of conduct. There are several different types. Generally, these include rules-based codes, principles-based codes, and comprehensive codes. Since every company's culture, business, and industry are different, it is important to adapt and personalize your corporate ethical code to your company's unique culture, personality, and business environment. The type of code your company adopts may be based on your company's relative size and stage of development. But your company can benefit from reading the corporate codes that have been adopted by other well-known and respected public companies, as well as those that have been adopted by your competitors.

Rules-Based Codes

A rules-based code is mostly focused on risk management and legal liability loss prevention. This type of code sets forth specifically designated rules, or "do's and don'ts," describing exactly how your employees should act when confronted with various different types of typical legal and ethical situations.

While it is not practical for your company to be able to foresee every potential illegal or unethical employee behavior, it should be relatively easy for your code to address the most typical and recurring legal and ethical dilemmas that happen in the daily conduct of your company's business. Specifically addressing the most common legal and ethical issues will make your code most useful in actually affecting your employees' behavior before it turns into misconduct.

Principles-Based Codes

A principles-based code of conduct focuses on establishing your company's general business values and cultural philosophy on how you want to do business and be perceived by your constituencies. These types of codes, often very brief, are also typically called "value statements" or "credos."

A principles-based code does not establish specific situational rules, but sets overarching general principles and expectations of ethical conduct and behavior that then can be generally applied by your employees to many different types of business situations.

Often this type of code stretches beyond ethical tenets to address broader core philosophies about how your company desires to do business and how it desires to be viewed by the world. Frequently included are your company's vision and mission statements and your guiding business principles.

Comprehensive Codes

Most codes of conduct are a combination of both general, broad-based principles of conduct and specific rules and procedures extrapolated from these core principles to apply to various specific situations. The example codes of conduct included in the appendices to this book are comprehensive in nature.

Ethical Programs Based on Your Company's Size

Daniel Kile, a noted author on ethical business conduct, has provided some useful rules of thumb in his book, *Business Conduct and Ethics: How to Set Up a Self-Governance Program,* for the type of corporate code of conduct and ethical program your company may consider adopting, depending upon how many employees your company has. According to Kile:

At 10 employees, your company should start drafting business principles.

At 50 employees, your company should adopt a written code of conduct and set up a business conduct and ethics steering committee to perform executive oversight on how your company's business is conducted.

At 200 employees, your company should begin organizing and formalizing your ethics program, including adopting a formal program of ethics communication, training, monitoring, and enforcement.

At 1,000 employees, your company should set up formal whistle-blowing procedures and an external hotline.

At 5,000 employees, your company should set up an internal hotline and ethics office.

Drafting Your Code

Setting the right tenor and tone in your written code of conduct is important to make sure your employees read and understand it. Your code must be written in plain English and in a manner that your employees can relate to and easily understand. Avoid legalese and technical jargon. Use the first person and an active voice as much as possible. Your code must be an active, living document. Keep your sentences short and to the point. Avoid compound sentences. Use bullet points and descriptive section headings. Make sure your code's policies and procedures are fact-specific and particularized to your company's unique business, operations, and industry. Include as many real-life applicable examples as possible to better illustrate the concepts and rules in your code.

While your code needs to be tailored to your company's unique fundamental values, some basic principles should be followed in drafting your corporate code.

Start broadly by describing your company's core values and guiding principles and philosophies about how your organization wants to conduct its business and be known to its constituencies.

Next, apply these fundamental values and principles to address your company's general business dealings and relationships with each of your company's core constituencies, including your customers, suppliers, employees, shareholders, communities in which your company operates, competitors, and your company itself. Adopt general principles for how you want your employees to treat and interact with each of your company's key constituencies. Then address specific examples of typical legal and ethical situations involving each constituency and how your employees should react to each situation.

Your general counsel or outside attorney should then address the main laws, regulations, and potential legal liabilities to which your company and employees are subject. Your code should specifically address how your employees should behave to avoid violating these laws or otherwise subjecting your company, board of directors, or management to prosecution, litigation, or legal liability.

If your company does business with governmental entities, you should incorporate each agency's unique ethical requirements.

Your company's code of conduct should establish your management's and supervisors' clear responsibility for monitoring and enforcing your standards of conduct throughout your business. All of your employees should be required and encouraged to report violations of your company's code of conduct, as well as any other perceived illegal or unethical behavior. The consequences of code violations and unethical or illegal actions should be clearly explained.

Finally, from a legal perspective, your code should make it clear that, while individual employee violations of your company's code are outside the scope of their employment and will result in individual sanction or even termination, your code is not intended to establish independent criteria for imposing legal liability on your company, board of directors, or management should there be an employee violation. You should also include a disclaimer in your company's code of conduct that your code does not constitute an employment contract or any guarantee of continued employment to your company's employees. Additionally, your code should state that its policies, guidelines, and related procedures are subject to unilateral change by your company at any time.

Generally, your corporate code should apply across the board to all of your employees. However, certain parts of your code will apply more to certain types of your employees, especially key employees, than others. For instance, the portion of your code that addresses financial statement and accounting integrity is obviously not particularly applicable to your production line employees. Your company may decide to have separate codes of conduct, sub-codes of conduct, or individual policy statements for different classes of employees or with respect to specific subject areas, such as your company's prohibitions against sexual harassment and discrimination or on your company's antitrust law compliance procedures. Similarly, you may decide to cover these types of topics in both your corporate code and in a separate policy statement on that specific type of behavior. This will help make sure your employees are well educated and informed on these particularly sensitive topics and high-risk areas.

While you may decide on distributing or stressing different parts of your code to different types of your employees, clearly the fundamental ethical values and principles of your company should be communicated to, and understood by, all of your employees throughout your entire organization.

Application to Contract Labor, Consultants, and Agents

The ethical values and rules that apply to your company's regular employees should apply equally to your part-time employees, contract labor, consultants, and agents. It should be the responsibility of your company's employees who retain a consultant, leased or temporary employee, or agent for any purpose to make sure they are well aware of your company's code of business conduct and that they agree to abide by all of its provisions.

Application to Union Employees

Depending on the terms and conditions of any collective bargaining agreements with your company's unionized employees and other applicable labor laws and regulations, the application of your company's code of conduct to your unionized workforce may be subject to bargaining with your union.

Communicating Your Code

Once your company's code of conduct has been finalized, it should be distributed with great fanfare and publicity throughout your company. Employees typically violate legal requirements and ethical standards either because they are ignorant of the applicable rules or they don't understand them. An effective communication and training program should help address both of these issues.

Preferably, your code should be broadly distributed to all of your employees along with a cover letter from your company's board of directors, CEO, or both (and your company's business owners, if your company is closely held) defining your company's core ethical values and explaining the importance of complying with your code. Many companies, particularly public companies, as now required by the Sarbanes-Oxley Act, publish their code of conduct on their company's Web site or Internet site.

If you have international operations, make sure you translate your code into the native language of your foreign-based employees.

After distribution, your code should be explained in detail to all of your company's employees at roll-out educational and training sessions. Employee attendance should be made mandatory at all levels. Your company may want to adjust the level and extent of education and training based on employee job functions and responsibilities. Your managers, supervisors, and other employees in sensitive positions (sales, marketing, finance, accounting, procurement, for example) may require more comprehensive ethics education and training than your rank-and-file employees. The extent of your company's ethics training program may depend on the size of your workforce and nature of your business. But, no matter what the size of your company, you should instruct all of your employees on ethical decision-making, as well as on the core principles of your code of conduct. Depending on the size of your company, these roll-out sessions can be videotaped or webcast to facilitate communication throughout your organization.

Your roll-out sessions should be led by your company's top management. They should involve discussion of your code's fundamental principles and values and how they apply to your company's various constituencies and to real-life situations that occur within your company and its business.

Try to maximize your employees' retention of your code's main messages by keeping your roll-out meetings interesting and fun. It is very important to effectively communicate your code of conduct to your employees. Role-playing or games on how to properly react to different ethical situations can be a great way to make your code take on real meaning to your employees.

After your roll-out sessions are completed, your employees should be asked to sign a statement that they have read and understand your code, and will comply with it. Such a requirement not only helps ensure that your employees do, in fact, read your corporate code of conduct, but it may also help your company to use these certifications to prove you have an effective compliance program. These certifications also can eliminate an employee's subsequent claim that he or she never knew about the ethical policies and procedures set forth in your code. (A certification can prove either that your employee did read and understand your policies or that he or she did not read and understand your code but lied when signing the certification).

Your company must be very consistent and diligent in maintaining records of these certifications. If you do a poor job of keeping track of these certifications, an employee who later violates your code, for example, but whose records do not contain the signed certification, may be able to use that fact to bolster the argument that he or she did not know the action was wrong. You may also want your employees to certify that they know of no existing code violations by others (and if they do, to disclose them) and that they will report violations they observe or become aware of.

Code of conduct implementation is expensive. Beyond the out-of-pocket cost of printing your code, the more significant costs will be the time and attention of your management team and employees spent to develop your code, paying your employees to attend your drafting and training sessions, and the associated opportunity cost of conducting these sessions.

After you've rolled out your code to all of your employees, the next step is distributing it to the outside world – to all of your company's key customers, vendors, communities, and others with whom your company does business. Companies are increasingly seeing the value of sharing their codes with their key customers, suppliers, business partners, lenders, and shareholders. Doing so can greatly enhance your company's reputation for integrity and the desirability of doing business with your company. This process will also help prevent your company's business partners from trying to corrupt your values and rules, particularly if they know you will stop doing business with them if they do so.

New Employees

As new employees join your company, they should be provided with a copy of your corporate code of conduct. Its application and importance should be stressed with each new employee by your human resources manager or your new employee's supervisor.

Each new employee should be required to view the videotape, CD-ROM, or Web site replay of your code of conduct roll-out session and training program. Many companies make their new employees take a test on their corporate code to make sure they've read and understood it. New employees should also be asked to sign a statement that they have read and understand your code, and will comply with it.

Refreshing Your Code

Continual communication is the key to effectively imprinting your code on the hearts and minds of your company's employees. Too often, corporate codes of conduct are initially adopted and even effectively rolled out with the best intentions, but after several years (or even months) they seem to be forgotten, and they lose importance and relevance in the minds of employees. Annual refresher training is critical to implementing an effective code of conduct and making a positive change in your employees' ethical behavior.

Your company's corporate code of conduct should also be reviewed and updated annually. This process will allow your code to be adapted to take into account your company's experiences in the application and enforcement of your code. It will also allow you to update your code to reflect changes in your company's markets, products, customers, and vendors. Your code of conduct must evolve with your company and with current events and circumstances. For example, the ethical collapses at Enron, WorldCom, and others resulted in many companies revisiting and updating their own codes of conduct and ethics training programs to ensure that the types of behavior experienced by those companies never happen at their company. Your code should also be updated at least annually to take into account changes in the law, as well as to incorporate new or more effective approaches to avoiding or solving ethical problems that have been experienced by your company's peers and competitors.

Promoting Your Code

Your corporate code of business conduct should be continuously promoted to your workforce.

Constant Awareness

Posters or signs on your company's bulletin boards and reminders in your company's newsletters or paycheck stubs are effective ways to keep your company's code in your employees' hearts and minds.

Many companies promote their codes in booklets distributed to all employees and post their codes on their Web sites or employee intranets. Laminated pocketbook cards containing your company's principal ethical philosophies can be given to your employees to help remind them regularly of these important company values. Many companies frame their core corporate conduct principles and philosophies and have them posted prominently throughout their facilities, particularly in their management's offices.

Ethical Compliance as Part of Performance Review

Make your employees' compliance with your ethical code of conduct an important part of their annual performance review. Code of conduct compliance and the practice of ethical conduct should be considered in any employee promotion or compensation decision, at least for your salaried employees. Similarly, your officers, supervisors, and managers should be held accountable for their departments' compliance with your code of conduct and for monitoring their subordinates' ethical business conduct.

3

ENFORCING YOUR CORPORATE CODE OF CONDUCT

Your company's code of ethical conduct will provide little, if any, tangible business benefits or effective legal protection to your company if it is not aggressively and consistently enforced and reinforced. Look no further than to Enron for an example. Enron had a wonderful written code of conduct (see Appendix). Obviously, however, it was neither followed nor enforced by Enron's senior management (Sherron Watkins excluded). If your company does not *live* your code, it won't be effective.

The process of enforcing and reinforcing your code can also serve the dual purpose of re-communicating your code's application and importance and educating your employees about proper legal and ethical behavior.

Starting at the Top, Again

Once again, enforcement and reinforcement of your company's code of conduct starts at the top, with your company's board of directors and CEO (and, if your company is closely held, its owners). Your employees will be much less likely to violate the law and your company's ethical rules and procedures if they are fully aware your company's management is very serious about enforcing your code and that compliance with it is one of your management's top priorities. This means your management must not only "talk the talk," but "walk the talk," as well.

It is very important that your management team does not turn a blind eye to legal or ethical code violations, even if – and especially if – the violations are committed by your directors, officers, managers, supervisors, or top-producing employees. Your management can't allow double standards of conduct to infiltrate your organization. Little things mean a lot. Your management can't tolerate or ignore unethical conduct, and they can't allow excellent results to justify illegal or unethical methods. If your employees see that other employees, particularly management and supervisory employees, who flaunt the rules still get promoted or praised (or don't get punished), then you'll have a very difficult time creating an organizational environment that will positively affect your employees' legal and ethical business behavior. Your company's managers need to be personally accountable for their ethical behavior too, as well as the ethical behavior of their subordinates.

Your company's management also cannot be oblivious to the conduct going on around them. Ignorance is not bliss. Your management and supervisors need to know how results are being generated by their subordinates. They must ask the right questions and get satisfactory answers. A high level of inquiry into and awareness of your employee's business conduct is required to ensure not only that your company punishes unethical behavior, but also that your company reinforces and rewards ethical behavior.

As part of your code's enforcement and reinforcement, it is important that your management team and supervisors take a special role in creating a highly ethical work environment. They must be role models, making ethics part of their everyday jobs and leading by clear example. They also must coach your employees on the importance of ethical integrity, so your employees know what to expect – and what your senior management expects. Your supervisors need to be accessible and open to answering questions on ethical issues and helping their subordinates make the right decisions for the right reasons.

Legal Benefits

To obtain legal liability protection from your corporate compliance code, you must be able to show that your company has taken the necessary steps not only to effectively communicate your company's code of conduct to your employees, but also to enforce its application. The precedential value of the consistent enforcement of your code can help significantly when trying to defend your company, board of directors, or management against vicarious liability from the illegal or unethical acts of your employees.

Enforcement Team

The primary role for enforcing your code should lie with your executive officer team, including particularly your general counsel and your human resources manager.

To be most effective, your corporate code should be monitored and enforced by a designated ethics compliance officer. This person should be a senior-level and widely respected officer of your company. Your general counsel or human resources manager should be good candidates. This person should be charged with ongoing oversight of your code as an important part of his or her job description and compensation.

Your ethics compliance officer should oversee and ensure the ongoing monitoring, compliance, enforcement, enhancement, and interpretation of your code. She or he needs to focus on consistent and effective enforcement and reinforcement and should also be the primary designated source to answer legal or ethical questions. Your compliance officer should also have reporting responsibility and accountability for code compliance and enforcement. This reporting responsibility should flow directly to your company's CEO and board of directors or a designated ethics committee.

Your compliance officer should also be responsible for assessing, and continually reassessing, your company's program and process for communicating, educating, and training your employees on legal and ethical behavior and code of conduct compliance. This continual evaluation process will help your code of conduct and ethics program become successful at positively affecting your employees' ethical and legal behavior and preventing ethical and legal violations.

Ethics Committee

Many companies have created an ethics committee that either acts as their company's designated ethics compliance officer or is the body to whom their company's ethics compliance officer directly reports. In either case, the ethics committee typically comprises respected senior-level officers from diverse backgrounds. Typically, an ethics committee might include your company's chief legal officer, chief financial officer, human resources manager, public relations officer, and a senior business person. In some instances, the ethics committee may also include one or two rank-and-file employees to bring a different perspective to the committee.

When the ethics compliance officer reports to the ethics committee, the committee generally acts in an oversight role over the compliance officer and as a sounding board and interpretive body for difficult issues or circumstances, including those that:

- Involve or reflect adversely on the integrity of your company's board of directors or management or your company's books, records, or accounts

- Endanger life, health, or safety

- Result in the prosecution of, litigation against, or significant loss or penalty to, your company

Your committee and compliance officer should meet regularly to review your company's code compliance and enforcement activities and to evaluate your compliance officer's performance. Your committee should also be responsible for annually reviewing your company's code and ethics training and compliance program for updates and enhancements.

Questions

Your company should implement a highly publicized, well understood, and easily accessible mechanism by which your employees can ask anonymous and confidential questions about potentially illegal or unethical activities occurring inside your company. Your company should strongly encourage your employees to ask questions about ethical rule interpretations and the application of your code to specific situations. Many gray areas fall outside of the law and the best drafted codes. It is important for your employees to understand that, when they are in doubt about possible illegal or unethical behavior or situations, they should ask. If they don't get an answer, then they should ask again.

Typically, your employees should ask these questions of their supervisors or your ethics compliance officer or ethics committee. For employees who feel uncomfortable asking these individuals, a mechanism and process should be in place so they can ask their question directly of a senior member of your ethics committee, your ethical ombudsman, or your internal or external ethics hotline.

Establishing a well publicized and strictly confidential process and mechanism for answering ethical questions will allow your company to prevent legal or ethical violations, reinforce your code of conduct, and improve its effectiveness.

Reporting Violations

Your company's code of conduct should require any employee having information on any situation or act that may constitute illegal activity or a breach of your company's code of conduct, or who has any question as to whether a situation or act may constitute illegal activity or a breach of your company's code of conduct, to promptly report the situation to their supervisor or your company's ethics compliance officer. This reporting requirement should include notification of any known future situation or act that could constitute illegal activity or a breach of your code. Your code should explain that if your employee is not comfortable discussing the situation with his or her supervisor or your ethics compliance officer, then he or she should discuss the matter with your ethics committee or ombudsman, another senior officer, or your company's board of directors.

To encourage your employees to report illegal activities and code violations, your corporate code should establish reporting procedures that provide your employees' assurance that their confidentiality and anonymity will be protected. It is often difficult for an employee to raise ethical issues with his or her own supervisor. Such an action can often compromise your employees' perceived team-player spirit. Allowing your employees to report unethical activities anonymously and confidentially to your ethics committee, higher management, or board of directors provides a safety valve to your employees. Independent internal and external ethics hotlines provide a similar safety valve, since their inherent anonymity should fully protect the reporting employee from retaliation or recrimination. Establishing a reporting system also can have protective benefits for your company under the Federal Sentencing Guidelines.

Your company's code of conduct should make it clear that no one will be allowed to interfere with this reporting mechanism or to retaliate against any reporter.

Additionally, your company's code of conduct should stress that no one is allowed to use your reporting system as a subterfuge to harm or slander another employee through false or misleading accusations or spreading disparaging rumors. Making false or misleading accusations should be made an explicit code violation in and of itself, subject to certain and consistent punishment.

Publicize well your ethical violation reporting mechanism throughout your company.

Investigating Allegations

Your employees' allegations of illegal or unethical activities or violations of your company's code of conduct need to be investigated. Your procedures should require an impartial and objective investigation into all plausible allegations. Confidential records of your inquiry process and its results need to be maintained for each case.

Typically, your inquiry process should start with a confidential interview of the reporting employee. This interview can often be performed anonymously, particularly if done over the telephone by a hotline operator or ombudsman.

The next phase should be a confidential interview of the alleged offender, who needs to be apprised of the allegations. The identity of the accuser must remain confidential. The investigator also should confidentially interview any others who witnessed, were involved in, or are aware of, the allegations.

The allegations will be either substantiated or unsubstantiated by your investigation. If the allegations are unsubstantiated, the matter should be closed; a record to that effect should be maintained; and the allegations should remain absolutely confidential. You may need to consider whether the allegations were made in good faith by the reporter or if there were ulterior motives. A heavy presumption of good faith should be accorded to the reporter, since you don't want to discourage your employees from reporting violations, or even perceived violations, of your company's code of conduct.

Of course, if the allegations are substantiated, the offender must be properly punished.

Punishing Violations

Violations of your company's code of conduct must be properly punished. Without disciplining illegal or unethical conduct, it will likely repeat itself, and your code of conduct will become ineffective. Punishment must be certain, consistent, and proportionate to the offense, after giving the alleged offending employee due process.

Similarly, the failure of your supervisors, ethics compliance officer, or ethics committee to detect illegal or unethical employee behavior should also be addressed. It is important for your company to require accountability for the oversight and proper monitoring and enforcement of your company's ethical rules.

Rewarding Compliance

Your top management should not only punish code violations, but they should also reward exemplary ethical behavior. Positive reinforcement of ethical behavior examples will set the stage for others to follow suit. It will also support and reinforce your employees' belief that ethics matter at your company. Don't be shy about publicizing to your employees great examples of how they should properly conduct their business affairs and interact with others. Whether you describe the good example in your company's newsletter or at an employee meeting, the public pat on the back will not only make the good-deed-doer feel good, but it will encourage your other employees to strive to receive compliments, too. For the best effect, make sure your CEO is the one handing out the public accolades.

Waivers

There may be times when your company's code of conduct needs to be waived for good business reasons to accommodate certain behavior that your code would otherwise prohibit. However, waivers of your code, especially if they involve your company's directors or senior officers, need to be subject to a rigorous review and approval process. The reasons for granting such a waiver need to clearly benefit your company, while not being inconsistent with your company's fundamental ethical business principles. Waivers should be very infrequent and should not repeatedly involve the same employee. Illegal behavior should never be allowed or waived.

Your ethics compliance officer or ethics committee should be the only parties with authority to grant a waiver to your regular employees. In instances involving a director or officer, only the disinterested members of your board of directors should approve the waiver. Under the Sarbanes-Oxley Act, code of conduct waivers granted to a director, senior officer, or financial officer of a public company must be publicly disclosed.

Keeping Records

It is important for your designated ethics compliance officer, general counsel, or human resources director to maintain excellent written records of your company's consistent punishment of employees' illegal activities and violations of your code. Proper documentation of these circumstances, as well as circumstances that did not merit punishment, and retention of these records will provide important, objective support for similarly punishing future instances of employee misconduct, as well as defending against potential company or management liability that could result from future or repeated employee transgressions.

Annual Review

Your company's code of conduct should be formally reviewed at least annually by your ethics compliance officer or ethics committee, as well as by your company's CEO and board of directors. This review should be more than perfunctory. It should include an active inquiry into and analysis of how effectively your company's code of conduct has been communicated to your employees, how well your employees have been educated and trained on ethical and legal conduct and compliance, and how well your code has been enforced and reinforced. Particular attention and review should be directed to any waivers of your code that may have been granted in the past year, particularly for senior officers or directors.

Transgressions of your code, particularly if they are repeated, should result in revisiting your code and your ethics training program to reassess whether further corrective action, training, or education needs to be undertaken to prevent future reoccurrences of the same illegal or unethical behavior.

Independent Audits

Depending upon the effectiveness of your company's annual formal code of conduct review process, your company should undergo a periodic independent "audit" of your ethics program and code of conduct enforcement by your company's outside lawyers or independent auditors. This independent audit should be undertaken after your first year of code implementation (or reimplementation), and then perhaps every other year thereafter.

This independent audit process will allow your company to obtain unbiased expert advice on how you may be able to improve your written code of conduct, your code's implementation and enforcement, and your legal and ethics educational and training program. Such an audit can allow your company to influence your employees' ethical behavior and legal and code compliance even more positively and effectively.

4
ETHICAL TREATMENT
OF YOUR CUSTOMERS

General Principles

A core element of your company's code of conduct should be establishing policies and procedures on how your employees should treat your customers and how your products and services should be marketed and sold. One of your company's primary goals that should be highlighted in your code is for your employees to deal with your customers lawfully, ethically, and fairly at all times, regardless of their relative size or importance.

One of the main benefits of a corporate code of conduct is to show evidence of your company's commitment, internally and externally, to providing excellent customer service and high-quality services and products to your customers at fair prices and in honest transactions. Your company more than likely prospers to the degree that your employees serve your customers well. In this regard, your corporate code of conduct can be used to emphasize to your employees that your company's customer appeal should be based on the quality, reliability, and safety of your company's products, the service with which your company supports them, the prices your company charges, and the competence and honesty of your product and sales presentations.

Your company's code of conduct should require your employees to provide accurate information to your customers so they can make fully informed purchasing decisions. Your code should not allow your employees to engage in any misrepresentation, fraud, or omission of information to your customers. Your code should emphasize that your company's advertising, packaging, and product labeling should never misrepresent the nature or value of your company's products and services.

Your code should also provide guidance and direction to your employees on how they should handle mistakes that are made with respect to your customers. Your code should stress the responsibility of your employees at all levels to respond promptly and positively to any customer complaint concerning your company's products or services.

Your company's code of conduct should make it clear that your employees should not try to "buy business" from your customers. In this regard, your code should prohibit your employees from providing cash, material gifts, trips, loans, or favors to your customers in an attempt to unduly influence their decision to buy your company's products or services.

If a government agency is a customer of your business, your code should include specific additional rules and policies on how your employees need to act to properly obtain and maintain government contracts in accordance with the applicable government contract procurement regulations, rules, and policies.

Customer Service and Quality

Your company's code of conduct should stress your commitment to excellent customer service. Your basic customer service principles and specific rules of behavior and examples should be set forth in your code. To provide even more specific direction to your company's employees, your code could also address various customer service situations that have occurred in the past at your company, and that may occur in the future. In each case, your code could describe how your employees should react to such situations in the interests of providing great customer service.

Your company's code of conduct should emphasize that your products and services should be marketed and sold to your customers based solely on their price, quality, service, and other competitive features.

Sales and Marketing Activities

Your company's employees should be allowed by your code of conduct to use only legal, ethical, and proper methods to sell and maintain the markets for your company's products and services. Your corporate code should specifically prohibit your employees from engaging in any of the following sales and marketing activities with your customers:

- Using deceptive or misleading statements
- Attempting to induce your customers to place their personal interests above those of their own companies
- Attempting to restrict competition with your company by:
    - Inducing a competitor or customer to breach a contract with a third party
    - Obtaining unauthorized access to classified or proprietary information or documents
    - Securing an unfair competitive advantage
- Violating any law, regulation, or rule
- Engaging in any activity that could damage your company's or your customer's reputation
- Engaging in sales or marketing activities that could embarrass your company, your employees, or your customers.

Fair Dealing With Customers

Your company's code of conduct should require your employees to deal with your customers in only a fair and impartial manner, regardless of their relative size or importance to your company. Business should be won or lost on the competitive merits of your company's products and services.

Offering Business Courtesies to Customers

To help ensure that your employees deal with your customers on a fair and impartial basis, your company's code of conduct should generally prohibit your employees from offering a "business courtesy" to a customer under any circumstances that might unduly influence their decision to purchase your company's goods and services, create the appearance of impropriety, or otherwise cause embarrassment to your company or your customer. In these situations, you may want your code to advise your employees to think about how the granting of a business courtesy might be viewed by a skeptical public reading about the granting of such courtesy in your local newspaper.

Generally, a "business courtesy" is a present, gift, gratuity, hospitality, or favor for which fair market value is not paid by the recipient. A business courtesy may be a tangible or an intangible benefit, including such items as gifts, meals, drinks, entertainment (including tickets and passes), recreation (including golf course and tennis court fees), door prizes, honoraria, transportation, discounts, promotional items, or use of a donor's time, materials, facilities, or equipment.

Your company's code should provide that any employee who offers or approves the offer of a business courtesy must ensure that it is ethical and proper in all respects, that the business courtesy cannot reasonably be interpreted as an attempt to gain an unfair business advantage or otherwise reflect negatively on the reputation of your company or your customer, and that the business courtesy does not violate your company's anti-kickback or bribery policy.

Generally, your code may allow your company's employees to offer business courtesies to customers only if the following four conditions are met:

- The business courtesy does not violate any law, regulation, or rule, or known corporate policy of the customer.

- The business courtesy is customary and consistent with the reasonable and ethical business practices of your industry and marketplace.

- Management or supervisor approval at an appropriate level is obtained.

- The cost to your company of the business courtesy is properly reflected on the books and records of your company and is reimbursable under your company's applicable ordinary and reasonable business expense reimbursement policies.

In deciding whether a business courtesy may be given to a customer, your code should provide your employees with specific guidance that considers and describes the circumstances surrounding the offer, the nature of the business courtesy, the appearance such an offer may create, and the value of the business courtesy. If the offering of a business courtesy could have an adverse impact on your company's or customer's reputation, your code should prohibit such an offer.

Entertainment or a gift purchased at your employee's own personal expense under circumstances that make it clear that the entertainment or gift is based solely on a personal friendship is generally not considered a business courtesy. These types of situations generally should not be prohibited by your corporate code. However, when both business and personal relationships exist between your employee and customer, these types of circumstances should be reviewed more closely by your company. In such cases, your company should still be sensitive to avoiding any personal activity or situation that could create an actual or apparent conflict of interest.

A more detailed discussion of this subject is found in Chapter 6.

Accounting for Business Courtesies

Your code should make it clear that your company's funds associated with an employee's offer of a business courtesy to a customer must be properly recorded on your company's books and records in accordance with your company's accounting procedures and practices.

Government Customers

If your company and employees deal with governmental agencies as customers, your corporate code of conduct should require them to have intimate knowledge of the laws, regulations, and agency-imposed rules and policies applicable to the sale or marketing of your company's products and services to that agency and its procurement process. In addition, ethics laws strictly regulate "business courtesies" to government personnel. To help ensure that your employees fully understand these strict requirements, your code should address and restate the rules and laws applicable to the government officials and employees in the jurisdictions with which your company does business.

Company's Interests Above Personal Interests

Your company's corporate code of conduct should prohibit your employees from engaging in activities that would induce or appear to induce employees or representatives of your customers to place their personal interests above those of their own company. In this regard, your code should prohibit your employees from engaging in the following activities:

- Offering or providing money, loans, gifts, or other favors that might appear to be designed to unduly influence your customer's business decisions or compromise the independent judgment of the employees or representatives of a customer

- Entering into various types of business relationships with the employees or representatives of a customer, such as joint ownership of property or personal financial relationships, that might place or appear to place the employees or representatives of your customer in a conflict of interest with their own company

- Offering or providing bribes, rebates, or kickbacks to the employees or representatives of a customer to obtain information or business for your company

Prohibited Conflict of Interest Activities

Your code of conduct should prohibit your employees from engaging in the following potential conflict of interest activities involving your company's customers, or at least require that your employees fully disclose such situations to a designated company official and receive your company's authorization to engage in such activities:

- Any significant investment, ownership interest (other than nominal amounts of stocks or bonds in publicly traded companies), or financial interest in any customer, particularly in a customer with respect to whom your employee can directly or indirectly influence contracts, processes, products, or services, or where your employee can influence your company's business decisions with respect to your customers

- Acting as an employee, officer, director, partner, consultant, representative, agent, or advisor, of a customer

- Having any personal financial involvement with an employee or representative of a customer, particularly if your employee regularly comes into contact with that individual while performing your company's business

- Participating in any activity that might lead to, or give the appearance of, unapproved disclosures of your company's confidential or proprietary information, or the confidential or proprietary information owned by your customers who have entrusted such information to your company

- Dealing directly, in the course of your employee's normal company responsibilities, with the employee's spouse or immediate family member who is employed by a customer of your company

Accurate Information to Your Customers

Your company's code of conduct should make it clear that information provided by your company's employees to your customers about your company's products or services should be accurate and free of misleading or deceptive statements or intentional omissions of material facts.

Similarly, your code should stress that your employees should make only those promises or commitments to your customers that they intend to and can keep in good faith. In the normal course of your company's business, if your company and its employees provide cost, delivery time, or other estimates to your customers, your code should emphasize that your employees should have a good-faith, reasonable basis for their estimates. In general, "reasonable" should mean based upon known facts in instances where facts exist, or upon the estimator's plausible and honest business judgment in the absence of facts.

Your code should also require that your company's product and service advertising and promotions always be truthful and accurate. Appropriate support or evidence to substantiate specific claims about your company's products or services or the performance of your company's products should be required by your code. Similarly, your code should exhibit your company's commitment to not labeling or marketing your company's products or services in any way that might mislead or cause confusion between your products or services and those of any of your competitors.

If your company offers advertising or promotional allowances, your company's code of conduct should require that your employees offer them on a proportionately equal basis to all of your customers.

Protecting Proprietary Information – Yours and Theirs

Your company's code of conduct should emphasize that your employees should not disclose your company's confidential and proprietary information to a customer or potential customer unless disclosure is expressly authorized by a designated company official and appropriate confidentiality protections are established with your customer.

Your corporate code should stress that your customers' confidential and proprietary information and resources should be protected by your employees to the same extent they should protect your own company's confidential and proprietary information and resources. Your employees should be made responsible by your company's code of conduct for complying with customer-imposed limitations governing the use of customer confidential information, including such items as documents, processes, practices, trade secrets, and computer software.

No Indirect Actions

Your company's code of conduct should prohibit your employees from asking others to do anything they are not permitted to do themselves under your company's code. Your code should also stress that an employee should never use personal funds or resources to do something that cannot be done with your company's resources.

Previous Relationships of Employees with Customers

Your employees who have been previously employed by a customer of your company should be required by your code to alert a designated company official to this fact. This will ensure that the employee's dealings with this customer are permissible under applicable rules and regulations and your customer's code of conduct. Your code should prohibit your employees' use of confidential or proprietary information of your customer to your customer's disadvantage.

For these reasons, you may want your code to prohibit an employee who previously worked for a customer from being directly involved in your company's business relationship with that customer – or at least not without appropriate authorization from a designated official at your company and your customer or a suitable "cooling-off" period.

5
ETHICAL TREATMENT
OF YOUR SUPPLIERS

General Principles

A principal tenet of your company's code of conduct should be establishing policies and procedures for how your employees should treat your company's suppliers and vendors and how they should purchase products and services from your suppliers and vendors. Your code should emphasize fair competition, without discrimination or deception, in a manner that creates long-lasting business relationships with your suppliers.

Your company's code of conduct should stress that your employees should deal with all of your suppliers fairly, honestly, and openly, regardless of their relative size or importance to your company. Your code should emphasize that your suppliers should be chosen without regard to the nationality of the supplier or the race, gender, or religious background of the supplier's owners. While it is a good business practice to select suppliers that reflect the diversity of your company's customer base (for example, minority and women-owned businesses), selections should still be based primarily on merit.

Your code should prohibit your employees from taking any action that would unduly influence or restrict your company's purchasing decisions. Procurement decisions by your employees should be made solely on the basis of quality, service, price, delivery, best value, and other similar competitive factors.

Your code should explain that your employees should exercise care to avoid actual and perceived conflicts of interest and the appearance of partiality or preferential treatment in all business transactions with your company's suppliers and vendors.

Your code of conduct should make it clear that your employees should not accept business courtesies, such as cash, material gifts, trips, loans, or other favors that would unduly influence their decision, or appear to unduly influence their decision, to purchase goods or services for your company.

Your code should generally prohibit your employees from accepting product discounts for personal purchases from your vendors or suppliers who otherwise provide goods or services to your company (unless the discounts are generally made available to others).

Your code should also prohibit or restrict your company from using suppliers whose employees include family members of employees of your company. This is particularly true when your employee's family member is involved in actively providing services or goods to your company or if your employee is involved in purchasing products or services from his or her relative who works for your supplier.

If your company contracts with the government, your code should require that your company's suppliers and vendors be aware of the special requirements of doing business with the government.

Accepting Business Courtesies from Suppliers

Your code of conduct should provide that all business courtesies offered to and accepted by your employees are property that belongs to your company. Your code should state that your employees do not have a right to keep a business courtesy from a supplier for personal benefit or use. In deciding whether to accept a business courtesy, your employees should be directed by your code to use good business judgment and to ask their supervisor or your company's ethics compliance officer when in doubt. Imposing these requirements should help promote professional relationships and practices with your suppliers and enhance your company's reputation for fairness and integrity.

A business courtesy generally is a present, gift, gratuity, hospitality, or favor from persons or firms with whom your company maintains or may establish a business relationship and for which fair market value is not paid by the recipient. A business courtesy may be a tangible or intangible benefit, including, for example, gifts, meals, drinks, entertainment (including tickets and passes), recreation (including golf course and tennis court fees), door prizes, honoraria, transportation, discounts, promotional items, and use of a donor's time, materials, facilities, or equipment.

Guidelines for Accepting a Business Courtesy From a Supplier

Your company's code of conduct should provide the following guidance to your employees on when they may keep a business courtesy from a supplier or vendor:

- If acceptance promotes a successful working relationship and goodwill with your company's suppliers or vendors.

- If the courtesy conforms to the reasonable and ethical practices of your business's industry and marketplace, such as flowers, fruit baskets, and other modest presents that commemorate a special occasion. Similarly, courtesies such as infrequent business meals and entertainment shared with the person who has offered to pay for them are also generally acceptable. But good judgment should be used, and invitations for meals and entertainment that are inappropriately lavish or excessive should be declined.

- If acceptance does not create an actual or perceived conflict of interest or divided loyalty, such as placing the interests of your company's suppliers or vendors that offered the courtesy above the interests of your company, including your company's interest in conducting business fairly and impartially and in treating all of your company's suppliers equally.

- If acceptance does not create the appearance of an improper attempt to influence your company's business decisions, such as accepting courtesies or entertainment from a supplier whose contract is expiring in the near future or who is bidding on a new contract.

- If the courtesy is a novelty, advertising, or promotional item of nominal value, such as calendars, pens, and mugs.

Your company's code should further specify that your employees who award contracts, influence the allocation of business, create product or service specifications for the placement of business, or participate in negotiating contracts should be particularly careful to avoid accepting courtesies that create the appearance of favoritism or that may adversely affect your company's reputation for impartiality and fair dealing with all of your company's suppliers. Your code should instruct your employees that the prudent course is to refuse a courtesy from a supplier when your company is choosing or reconfirming a supplier or under circumstances that would otherwise create an impression that offering courtesies is the way for suppliers to obtain your company's business.

It is not uncommon for people in business relationships to further those relationships in a social setting – meals, attendance at sporting events, concerts, or other cultural events, or participation in recreational activities, such as a round of golf or a game of tennis. On those occasions, one party typically provides or pays for the meal, entertainment, or recreation of the other. Generally, your code of conduct may allow your employees to participate in these activities, provided attendance includes both your company's employee and external business associates, the entertainment is not lavish, and those offers are made only on an infrequent basis.

Other typical circumstances involve entertainment and recreational activities that are offered by a supplier in connection with out-of-town business travel. Generally, your company's code of conduct may allow these types of courtesies to be accepted, as long as the entertainment or recreation is only incidental to travel that otherwise involves a substantial business purpose. As a general rule, your code of conduct should prohibit your employees from accepting a trip offered by a supplier without any "substantial business purpose," or in which entertainment or recreation would be the principal activity. In addition, your code of conduct may provide that an out-of-town trip intended primarily to foster a business relationship does not amount to a "substantial business purpose" for accepting entertainment and recreation.

On occasion, an employee of your company may be invited to an out-of-town meeting, seminar, or site visit by a supplier or vendor doing business, or seeking to do business, with your company. In general, your code of conduct should provide that accepting transportation and lodging paid for by a supplier is improper. A good rule of thumb for your code to consider is that if the travel is for legitimate company business, your company should pay; if not, your employee should decline the invitation. But, in connection with a business trip, if an offer is received to stay with a friend who also happens to be a business counterpart, your code may provide that the offer may be accepted when to refuse to do so would appear discourteous, and the offer could not reasonably be considered to be made to influence your employee's business judgment.

Your company's code of conduct should provide that accepting gifts or favors offered because of services performed on behalf of your company, your employee's position at your company, or a business relationship your company has or that is being proposed, is generally improper. Nothing should be accepted that could reasonably be considered to influence your employees' judgment in regard to the affairs of your company.

Similarly, your company's code should state that prize drawings, such as door prizes at events sponsored by vendors or others seeking to do business with your company, may be accepted by your employees only if eligibility is open to anyone in attendance, attendance goes beyond your company's employees, and it is truly a prize -- that is, it is based on chance, and not everyone gets a prize.

Certain gifts, by their nature, are inappropriate because they cannot avoid raising at least the appearance of a conflict of interest for the recipient. These include cash and cash equivalents (such as gift certificates for meals, recreation, merchandise, or other property or services; things convertible to cash, such as bonds or marketable securities; and discounts on merchandise). Acceptance of these gifts, even if of nominal value, should be prohibited by your code.

In addition, gifts delivered to an employee's home or given to members of the employee's family are generally improper and should be prohibited by your code.

Your company's code of conduct should also prohibit your employees from engaging in a pattern of accepting frequent courtesies from the same supplier or vendor.

In short, your company's code should prohibit your employees from accepting courtesies from suppliers or vendors that they would not feel comfortable discussing with their manager, coworkers, or a member of the media.

Unacceptable Actions

Your company's code of conduct should prohibit your employees from engaging in the following actions with your company's vendors and suppliers:

- Asking for a business courtesy
- Accepting a business courtesy when:
  - Your supplier or vendor is offering the courtesy in exchange for, or to influence, favorable action by your company
  - Your supplier or vendor is attempting to motivate your employee to take an action that is prohibited by law, regulation, or company or supplier policy
  - Your supplier or vendor is attempting to gain an unfair competitive advantage by improperly influencing your employee's discretionary procurement decisions
- Using your position at your company as a means of obtaining business courtesies, such as personal discounts that are not generally made available to others on products, services, or other items of value from your company's customers or suppliers
- Accepting offers of expense-paid trips for pleasure from your company's vendors or suppliers

Guidelines for Disposition of Unacceptable Business Courtesies

Your company's code should provide the following guidelines for how your employees should dispose of an unacceptable business courtesy received from suppliers or vendors:

- Return it to your supplier or vendor with a polite explanation that your company's policy prohibits keeping it.

- Promptly forward the courtesy to a company-designated charitable, civic, or educational organization.

- Retain the courtesy for display purposes only, with the approval of your company's ethics compliance officer.

- Retain the courtesy for personal benefit or use with the approval of your company's ethics compliance officer, if your employee pays your company an amount equal to the fair value of the business courtesy.

When local customs or practices make it inappropriate to decline the business courtesy at the time it is offered, your employee should initially accept the courtesy and then later follow your company's guidelines for disposition.

Prohibited Conflict of Interest Activities

Your company's code of conduct should prohibit your employees from engaging in the following activities with or involving your company's suppliers or vendors (or at least require that your employees fully disclose these situations to a designated company official and receive authorization to engage in such activities, which pose a potential conflict of interest):

- Any significant investment, ownership interest (other than nominal amounts of stocks or bonds in publicly traded companies) or financial interest in any supplier, particularly one with which your employee can directly or indirectly influence contracts, processes, products, or services of the supplier, or where your employee can influence your company's business decisions with respect to that supplier

- Acting as an employee, officer, director, partner, consultant, representative, agent, or advisor of a supplier to your company

- Having any financial involvement with an employee or representative of a supplier, particularly if your employee regularly comes into contact with this individual while performing your company's business

- Participating in any activity that might lead to or give the appearance of unapproved disclosures of your company's confidential or proprietary information, or the confidential or proprietary information owned by your suppliers who have entrusted such information to your company

- Dealing directly, in the course of your employee's normal company responsibilities, with the employee's spouse or immediate family member who is employed by a supplier to your company

No Kickbacks

Your company's code of conduct should strictly prohibit your employees from engaging in any of the following actions with your company's suppliers or vendors:

- Providing, attempting to provide, or offering to provide, any kickback

- Soliciting, accepting, or attempting to accept, any kickback

- Including, directly or indirectly, the amount of any kickback in the price charged

The term "kickback" generally includes any money, fee, rebate, commission, credit, gift, gratuity, thing of value, or compensation of any kind that is provided directly or indirectly to anyone for the purpose of improperly obtaining or rewarding favorable treatment in connection with a contract.

Foreign Suppliers

If your company purchases goods or services internationally, your code of conduct may consider requiring your company's foreign suppliers to follow workplace standards and business practices consistent with your company's standards and practices. A particular focus lately has been on companies requiring their suppliers to not engage in harsh or inhumane labor practices that would be considered unacceptable or illegal in this country.

Additional discussion of this subject is in Chapter 14.

Government as a Supplier

If a government entity is a supplier to your company, your code of conduct should require your employees to be intimately familiar with the various laws, regulations, and requirements that must be followed when dealing with a governmental agency. As a general rule, your employees cannot provide anything of value to government officials.

Protecting Proprietary Information – Yours and Theirs

Your company's code of conduct should emphasize that your employees should not disclose your company's confidential or proprietary information to a supplier or potential supplier unless disclosure is expressly authorized by a designated company official, and appropriate confidentiality protections are established with your supplier.

Your company's code of conduct should also emphasize that your employees should not disclose your supplier's confidential or proprietary information to any outside third party.

Your corporate code should stress that your employees should protect your supplier's confidential and proprietary information and resources to the same extent they should protect your company's confidential and proprietary information and resources. Your employees should be made responsible by your company's code of conduct for complying with supplier-imposed limitations governing the use of the supplier's confidential information, including such items as documents and computer software.

Indirect Actions

Your company's code of conduct should prohibit your employees from requesting others to do anything that they are not permitted to do themselves under your company's code.

Similarly, your code should also stress that an employee should never use personal funds or resources to do something that cannot be done with your company's resources.

Previous Relationships of Employees with Suppliers

Your employees who have been previously employed by a supplier of your company should be required by your company's code of conduct to alert a designated company official to this fact to ensure that their dealings with this supplier are permissible under applicable rules and regulations and your supplier's code of conduct. Similarly, your code should prohibit your employees' use of your supplier's confidential or proprietary information to your supplier's disadvantage.

For these reasons, you may want your code to prohibit an employee who was previously an employee of a supplier from being directly involved in your company's business relationship with that supplier – at least not without appropriate authorization from a designated official at your company and your supplier or a suitable "cooling off" period.

6

ETHICAL TREATMENT OF YOUR COMPANY

General Principles

Your company's corporate code of conduct should make it clear that your employees owe a duty of loyalty to your company. Your company has the right to expect the unfailing allegiance of your employees. Your employees must put your company's business interests above their personal self-interests when dealing with issues, transactions, and opportunities that may present an actual or perceived conflict of interest between them and your company or that present a corporate opportunity for your company.

Your company's code should generally prohibit your employees from:

- Allowing their personal interests to conflict with the best interests of your company
- Taking advantage of a business opportunity for their personal benefit without first offering your company every chance to take advantage of the opportunity
- Competing with your company or otherwise acting to your company's disadvantage

Your company's code should also require the devotion of your employees' business time and attention to your company. While your employees' rights to engage in private activities should always be respected, their ability to take a second job or engage in other private activities during their off-work hours should be prohibited, or at least strictly limited, if those activities would adversely affect the performance of their own job at your company, or disadvantage or embarrass your company.

Conflicts of Interest

Your company's transactions with other business entities should not be influenced by the personal interests or activities of your company's employees. A conflict of interest generally occurs when an employee's private interests interfere in any way – or even appear to interfere – with your company's business interests.

Conflict situations may arise when your employees take actions or have interests that may make it difficult for them to perform their jobs objectively or effectively or that otherwise may harm or disadvantage your company. Conflicts of interest also may arise when your employees or members of their families receive improper personal benefits as a result of their positions in your company. These conflicts may appear as favoritism or may otherwise damage the reputation of your company or your employees for integrity and impartiality.

An actual conflict of interest need not be present to constitute a violation of your company's code of conduct. Your company's code should specify that activities by your employees that create *even the appearance of a conflict of interest* should also be avoided to avoid negative reflection on your company's reputation.

Prohibited Conflict of Interest Activities

Your code should prohibit your employees from engaging in the following potential conflict of interest activities, or at least require your employees to fully disclose these situations to a designated company official and receive authorization to engage in them:

- Any significant investment, ownership interest (other than nominal amounts of stocks or bonds in publicly traded companies), or financial interest in any supplier, customer, or competitor, particularly those for whom your employee can directly or indirectly influence contracts, processes, products, or services, or for whom your employee can influence your company's business decisions

- Acting as an employee, officer, director, partner, consultant, representative, agent, or advisor, of any of the following:

  - A supplier, customer, partner, subcontractor, or competitor of your company

  - Any business involved in technical areas or product lines that are similar to, or competitive with, those of your company

  - Any business whose customers include your company, its customers, or its suppliers

- Receiving business courtesies from any company with which your company has business dealings, other than commonly distributed items of nominal value given for novelty, advertising, or promotions and conforming to customary industry or local market practices

- Outside activity that is so substantial as to adversely affect, or call into question, your employees' ability to devote their appropriate business time and attention to their job responsibilities with your company

- Being in the position of supervising, reviewing, or influencing the job evaluation, pay, or benefits of any close relative

- Using for personal gain, or personal benefit of others, confidential information obtained during or as a result of their employment with your company

- Taking personal advantage of a business opportunity that was learned of in the course of their employment with your company (at least without first giving your company the opportunity to take advantage of the opportunity)

- Personally buying or selling anything from or to your company, or any supplier or customer, except on terms and conditions generally available to non-employees or pursuant to any normal discount program offered to all employees in general

- Acquiring or holding an investment in real estate or other property in which your company may have an existing business interest or in which your employee has knowledge of your company's possible business interest
- Acting as a consultant, an advisor, or an expert witness in a legal process, such as a lawsuit, administrative proceeding, mediation, arbitration, dispute resolution, government or private investigation, rule-making procedure, or similar legal process
- Engaging in any activity that could create the appearance of a conflict of interest of your company and thereby impair the reputation of your company for integrity, impartiality, and fair dealing – for example:

  - Having any financial involvement with an employee or representative of a supplier, vendor, customer, partner, subcontractor, or competitor of your company with whom your employee regularly comes in contact while performing your company's business

  - Participating in any activity that might lead to or give the appearance of unapproved disclosures of your company's proprietary or confidential information, processes, or trade secrets, or of the proprietary or confidential information, processes, or trade secrets owned by others who have entrusted such information to your company

  - Accepting loans from persons or companies doing business with, or seeking to do business with, your company, except from recognized financial institutions, and then only at prevailing rates and terms and without using the employee's company connection to influence the loan

  - Dealing directly, in the course of your employee's normal company responsibilities, with the employee's spouse or immediate family member who is employed by a supplier, vendor, customer, or competitor of your company

If a situation or circumstance presents a direct conflict of interest for your employee, your company's code of conduct should also prohibit your employee's family or close relatives from engaging in such activity.

Activities That Generally Are Not Conflicts of Interest

Your company's code of conduct should consider advising your employees that the following activities are typically not considered prohibited conflict of interest activities:

- For your non-salaried employees, working during the employee's off-hours for any entity that is not a supplier, customer, competitor, partner, or subcontractor of your company, and is otherwise not involved in any technical areas or product lines similar to those of your company, provided the activity does not violate any other prohibition in your code (such as an anti-moonlighting policy) or otherwise adversely affect your employee's ability to objectively and effectively perform his or her job or create the potential to disadvantage, harm, or embarrass your company

- Participation, at the request of your company, in nonprofit professional, industry, educational, civic, or charitable activities or organizations (such as United Way)

- Certain passive investment interests, such as owning less than a small percentage of stock of a publicly traded company or having a normal, ordinary checking account, savings account, or borrowing relationship with a financial institution (even if the financial institution is a customer of, or lender to, your company)

Conflicts of Interest Disclosure Statements

Your code of conduct should annually require your employees to submit a formal written statement to your company disclosing any information known to them about the possible occurrence of a conflict of interest by them or any other employee in the past year. These statements, if properly reviewed, acted upon, and retained, can be very effective in (at least after the fact) identifying and properly addressing past or existing conflicts of interest. They also can be used as strong reminders to your employees about your company's conflict of interest policy. Finally, if any of your employees ever submits his or her annual conflicts disclosure statement and does not identify an existing conflict, once the conflict is discovered, the failure to have disclosed the situation may be grounds for imposing a harsher sanction on the employee.

Corporate Opportunities

Your employees owe your company a duty to advance its business interests when the opportunity to do so arises. Your code should prohibit your employees from taking personal advantage of business opportunities your company may be interested in. This "corporate opportunity doctrine" is complicated, and it may not be possible for your code to clearly define all of the specific business opportunities that belong, or could be of interest, to your company and what kinds of business opportunities your employees may take personal advantage of. Generally, however, your code of conduct should prohibit your employees from:

- Taking personal advantage of a business opportunity that typically would be pursued by, or would be of interest to, your company

- Taking personal advantage of any other business opportunity your company may want to take advantage of if the opportunity is discovered by your employee using company property, business contacts, or information, or that your employee becomes aware of because he or she works for your company

- Competing with or otherwise disadvantaging your company

Related-Party Transactions

Generally, your company's code of conduct should provide that your employees, and in particular your company's directors and officers, should not engage in a related-party transaction with your company, at least without full disclosure and authorization. Related parties are parties who may not deal with one another at arm's length, including:

- Any director, officer, or significant owner of your company

- Any organization in which a director, officer, employee, or significant owner of your company is also a director, officer, employee, or significant owner

- Any organization in which a director, officer, employee, or significant owner of your company is an owner or investor (other than owning less than a small percentage interest in a publicly traded company)

- Any trust in which a director, officer, employee, or significant owner of your company has a substantial interest or serves as trustee or in a similar fiduciary capacity

- Any relative of a director, officer, employee, or significant owner of your company who may significantly influence or be influenced by a business transaction with an organization in which he or she is a director, officer, employee, or significant owner

Your code should require any director, officer, employee, or significant owner who proposes to engage in a related-party transaction with your company, or who believes such a transaction exists or might occur, to inform your company's ethics compliance officer or board of directors as soon as possible. In certain instances, related-party transactions with your company may be allowed, as long as they are fully disclosed up front, are properly approved, provide your company with a clear business benefit, are fair and reasonable to your company, and are on terms and conditions no less favorable to your company than could be obtained from a similarly qualified, independent third party.

Loans from the Company to Directors and Executive Officers

In accordance with the prohibitions set forth in the Sarbanes-Oxley Act, if your company is publicly traded, your company's code of conduct should prohibit loans or extensions of credit (or the arrangement of extensions of credit) to your company's directors and executive officers. Even if your company is not publicly traded, since these types of transactions (particularly if your company is not in the business of providing loans or extending credit) raise related-party and conflict-of-interest concerns, your company's code of conduct should at least require that such transactions provide a clear business benefit to your company and are fully disclosed to and approved by your company's ethics compliance officer or your company's board of directors.

Devotion of Time and Ability to Your Company's Business

Your company should respect the rights of your employees to engage in activities of a private nature outside of their job responsibilities to your company. However, personal business interests or commitments by your employees should be prohibited by your company's code of conduct if those activities would impair your employees' ability to meet their regular job responsibilities to your company, would otherwise adversely affect their objectivity or effectiveness in carrying out their employment-related responsibilities, or would disadvantage, harm, or cause embarrassment to your company. Your code should require that any outside personal business interests or commitments of your company's full-time employees should receive the approval of your company's ethics compliance officer.

Outside Employment

Your code should prohibit your company's employees from engaging in any outside employment activities while on duty at your company. Your code should prohibit your employees from working for another employee during off-work hours if the other job would conflict with your company's interests, would adversely affect the objectivity or effectiveness of your employee in performing his or her duties for your company, or would disadvantage, harm, or cause embarrassment to your company. Your code should make this prohibition particularly applicable to your salaried employees.

As to the performance of any otherwise permissible outside work, your company's code of conduct should also prohibit your employees from engaging in any activity that would detract from their job performance or require such long hours as to adversely affect their physical or mental effectiveness. Similarly, your corporate code should not allow your employees to perform services for another entity if they would reflect adversely upon the integrity or reputation of your company.

Private Outside Activities

Your code should prohibit your company's employees from engaging in outside private activities while on duty at your company. These activities should not be allowed during off-duty hours if they would conflict with your company's interests, adversely affect the objectivity or effectiveness of your employees in performing their duties for your company, or otherwise disadvantage, harm, or cause embarrassment to your company.

For example, the chairman and CEO of a public company, who was also active in his local community, was publicly castigated for personally signing a petition of support of, and sending a relatively small personal contribution to, an organization opposed to the United States' declared war on terrorism and proposed military intervention against Iraq. While there is no question that the CEO had every personal right to express his personal political conscience in the way he did, his actions became a public maelstrom that questioned his patriotism, embarrassed his company, its shareholders, employees, and customers, and undermined his position and responsibilities both at his company and in his community.

Similarly, while your employees may have the private legal right to join such organizations as the Ku Klux Klan or a neo-Nazi group, your employees' association with such organizations clearly could bring scorn and embarrassment on your company.

Romantic Relationships with Other Company Employees

Your company's code of conduct should explain that romantic relationships between any of your company's employees and their supervisors or similar reporting person can lead to a loss of trust and confidence in the objectivity and fairness of the supervising employee. These relationships can also pose potential conflict of interest issues and create the appearance of favoritism, partiality, and discrimination among subordinates. Such relationships also risk the strong potential for sexual harassment or discrimination claims against the supervisor and your company, particularly when the romantic relationship ceases. For these reasons, your company's code of conduct should prohibit romantic relationships between a supervisor and his or her subordinate.

As a less desirable alternative, your company's code should at least require that these relationships be disclosed to an appropriate company official. Typically if such relationships are allowed, both the supervisor and the employee should sign a consent and waiver form indicating that their relationship is mutually consensual and that each party waives his or her rights to later claim sexual harassment or discrimination against the supervisor and your company as a result of the relationship.

Proper Use of Company Property

Your company's code of conduct should provide guidance to your employees on their proper use of your company's property. Your company's property, including your company's physical property, vehicles, office equipment, supplies, time, information, and intellectual property, are generally provided to your employees exclusively for their use in advancing your company's business. As a result, your company's code should generally restrict your employees' use of your company's property for non-company purposes.

Specifically, your company's code of conduct should require your employees, when using your company's resources, equipment, vehicles, and other property, to ensure that:

- Your company's resources, equipment, and other property remain on your company's property, unless use in another location has been authorized by a designated company official

- Company, customer, and supplier resources, equipment, and other property are not used by your employees for outside business activities or unauthorized purposes

- Resources, equipment, and other property entrusted to your company by current or prospective suppliers or customers are to be used by your employees only as specifically authorized by your company's supplier or customer

General Rules on the Personal Use of Company Property

Since your company may incur additional costs or disruption to its business from your employees' personal use of your company's property, your code may allow occasional personal use of company property, subject to the following guidelines:

- The personal use should be infrequent and minimal.

- The personal use must not be related to any illegal or unethical activity or the conduct of an outside business.

- The personal use must not disadvantage, harm, or cause embarrassment to your company.

- The personal use should not be in support of any religious, political, or other outside organizational activity, except for company-requested support to charitable, nonprofit, or educational organizations.

- The property should be used for personal purposes only on an off-hour basis, such as during lunchtime or before or after work hours.

- Proper measures are taken for the storage and safeguarding of your company's confidential or proprietary data and information to prevent unauthorized access, use, or removal by any means and in any form (electrical, optical, magnetic, or hardcopy) of such data or information.

- Any personal use of your company's computers or computer system does not compromise the security or integrity of your company's proprietary or confidential information or information systems.

- The personal use must not interfere with the performance of your company's business, your employee's assigned duties, or the assigned duties of other employees, and should not adversely affect the performance of your employees or your company.

- There should be no significant incremental cost to your company from such personal use, such as long-distance telephone charges.

Proper Use of Electronic Media, Equipment, and Services

As a result of the increasing importance and use of electronic forms of communication and information exchange in today's business world, in addition to your company's general rules on your employees' proper use of its property, it is important for your company's code of conduct to specifically address your employees' proper use of its electronic media, equipment, and services, such as computers, email, telephones, voicemail, fax machines, external electronic bulletin boards, wire services, online services, and the Internet. Your company should generally encourage the use of these electronic media, equipment, and associated services because information technology advances are making communication more efficient and effective, and because they are valuable sources of information about vendors, customers, new products, and services. But, your code of conduct should make it clear that company-provided access to electronic media, equipment, and services (for instance, an Internet account) are your company's property, and their purpose is to facilitate your company's business.

Because of the rapidly changing nature of electronic media, and because "netiquette" is developing and evolving on an ongoing basis among users of external online services and the Internet, it may be difficult for your company's code of conduct to cover every situation applicable to your business and your electronic media systems and equipment. Nonetheless, your company's code should set forth certain general principles to be applied and followed by your employees in their use of your company's electronic media, equipment, and services.

Your company's code should make it clear that your employees' use of your company-provided access to the Internet is intended to be primarily for your company's business-related purposes, including the communication, transmission, processing, and storage of company-authorized information. While your code can recognize that limited, occasional, or incidental use of electronic media (sending or receiving) for personal, non-business purposes is understandable and acceptable – as is the case with personal phone calls – your company's employees need to demonstrate a sense of responsibility and should not abuse the privilege. Your employees should be made aware that their company-provided Internet access may be monitored and their actual Website connections recorded. Your code should explain that excessive use of company-provided access to the Internet for non-business-related purposes will result in your employees' loss of access privileges or further disciplinary action.

Your company's email and voicemail systems should be used by your employees primarily for their job-related communications. While your company should respect the individual privacy of your employees for their personal affairs, your company's code of conduct should make it clear that these privacy rights and expectations do not extend to their work-related conduct or to their personal email or voicemail messages either sent or received on your company's systems.

In particular, your employees need to understand that your company's telephone, computer, voicemail, email, and Internet systems are not private, but instead are the property of your company. Making this point clear to your employees in your company's code of conduct is important if your company wants to be able to access your employees' email and voicemail and to also act as a check to deter sexual and other forms of harassment and discrimination in your company's workplace. Although your employees will likely each have their own individual password to access your company's voicemail or email system, your company's code of conduct should make it clear that the contents of voicemail, email, and Internet communications are accessible at all times by your company for any business purpose.

While your company's code of conduct may permit incidental and occasional personal use of your company's voicemail, email, and Internet systems, it should clearly state that such uses are treated the same as other uses, and that your company reserves the right to access and disclose all messages transmitted via your company's voicemail, email, and Internet systems, regardless of content. Your code should therefore prohibit your employees from ever using your communication systems to transmit a message they would not want read by a third party.

Your company's email, voicemail, and Internet policy should be adapted to fit your culture; the capabilities of your email software, voicemail, and Internet programs; the existence of your network linking employees' home computers to your workplace network; and your policies with regard to records retention.

Email messages may remain part of your company's business records long after they have been supposedly deleted. The resulting potential for adverse consequences to your company has never been more clearly illustrated than in the several situations that occurred in late 2002 and early 2003 at certain major Wall Street brokerage firms. Several very prominent Wall Street investment and research analysts were caught sending personal emails to their colleagues that denigrated the stocks of companies they were recommending to the public. As a result, those analysts and their firms were subject to significant fines and other penalties. Your company's code of conduct should stress that personal employee email use must not adversely affect your company or its public image or that of your customers or suppliers.

Additionally, your code should make it clear that your company's email should not be used for external broadcast messages or to send or post chain letters, messages of a political or religious nature, or messages that contain obscene, pornographic, profane, or otherwise offensive language, graphics, pictures, or material that otherwise violates your company's policies or procedures. Specific examples of transmissions that should be forbidden by your code include sexually explicit messages, graphics, pictures, cartoons, or jokes; unwelcome propositions or love letters; ethnic or racial slurs; and any other message that could be construed as harassing or disparaging of others on the basis of sex, race, religion, national origin, age, sexual orientation, or disability.

With respect to your employees' use of your company's electronic media, services, and equipment, your code of conduct should provide for the following rules:

- Your company's employees are responsible for the security of their account passwords and will be held responsible for all use or misuse of their accounts. They must maintain secure passwords to their accounts. Employees accessing the Internet over your company's network may be required to use an ID and password at the firewall (in addition to their usual LAN sign on). Employees must follow all directions of your company's system administrators with respect to security of passwords and take reasonable precautions against unauthorized access.

- Remote login to your company's network may be prohibited, unless permission to do so is granted. Your employees may be restricted from remotely logging into (or otherwise using) any workstation or computer not designated explicitly for public login over your company's network – even if the configuration of your company's computer permits remote access – unless your employees have explicit permission from the owner and the current user of that computer to log into that machine.

- Your employees may not use any account set up for another employee or attempt to find out the password of a service for which that employee does not have authorization, including accounts set up for other employees.

- Network services and World Wide Web sites can and do monitor access and usage and can identify at least the company – and often the specific individual – accessing their services. Thus, accessing a particular bulletin board or Web site leaves company-identifiable electronic "tracks," even if your company's employee merely reviews or downloads the material and does not post any message. Therefore, as a general rule, all of your company's employees' Internet use should be conducted with this in mind so they always portray your company's reputation and goodwill.

- Access to selected Internet hosts or networks that your company designates as inappropriate may be denied.

- Use of games or other non-work-related objects over the Internet should be prohibited.

Your company's employees may not use your company's electronic media for knowingly transmitting, retrieving, or storing any communication that is:

- Discriminatory, harassing, or threatening

- Derogatory or disparaging to any individual

- Obscene, pornographic, profane, sexually explicit, or offensive

- Defamatory

- An ethnic or racial slur

- A "chain letter" or junk mail

- Political or religious in nature
- Untrue or fraudulent
- Illegal or against your company's policy or contrary to your company's interest
- For personal profit

In downloading any material from the World Wide Web or by file transfer, or in distributing any material by email or file transfer, your employees must bear in mind any proprietary or intellectual property rights of third parties in the material. Your employees should not be allowed by your company's code to copy material when doing so would infringe the proprietary or intellectual property rights of third parties. This infringement is an offense that may render your employees and your company liable for civil claims and, where appropriate, may also be a criminal offense.

Your company's employees may not download or store any indecent or obscene material from the World Wide Web, or any such material received by email or by file transfer, and may not distribute any such material by file transfer or by email.

Your employees should not be allowed to send email or other electronic communications that attempt to hide the identity of the sender or represent the sender as someone else or as someone from another company. Your employees' names, their user IDs, and your company's name should be included in all email messages. Your employees are solely responsible for all electronic mail originating from their user IDs.

When using your company's email facilities, the following are prohibited:

- Forgery or attempted forgery of email messages
- Reading, deleting, copying, or modifying the email of others

Your company's employees must respect the confidentiality of other people's electronic communications and should not attempt to:

- "Hack" into third-party systems
- Read other people's logins or "crack" passwords
- Breach computer or network security measures
- Intercept or monitor electronic files or communications of other employees or third parties, except by explicit direction of your company's management

Many software programs and computer data and related materials, such as documentation, are owned by individual users or other companies and are protected by copyright and other laws, together with licenses and other contractual arrangements. Any of your company's employees who obtain electronic access to another company's or individual's materials must respect all rights (including copyrights) therein and should not copy, retrieve, modify, disclose, examine, rename, or forward such materials, except as permitted by the person owning the data, software programs, or other materials. Such restrictions should include:

- Copying programs or data
- Reselling programs or data

- Using programs or data for non-company business purposes
- Using programs or data for personal financial gain
- Using programs or data without being one of the licensed individuals or groups
- Publicly disclosing information about software programs without the owner's permission

In connection with enforcing your code's policies and rules on the proper use of its electronic media, equipment, and systems, you may decide to monitor all electronic information created and/or communicated by an employee using email, word processing, utility programs, spreadsheets, voicemail, telephones, and Internet and Bulletin Board System access. You may consider routinely monitoring usage patterns for both voice and data communications (for example, number called or site accessed; call length; times of day when calls were initiated) for cost analysis and allocation and the management of your access to the Internet. You also may reserve the right to review and disclose any electronic files and messages (including email) and usage to the extent necessary to ensure that your company's electronic media, equipment, and services are being used in compliance with its code and the law. You may also find it necessary to monitor your company's systems for signs of illegal or unauthorized entry, so your employees should be required to waive any right to privacy in such electronic files. Your employees should understand that electronic communications are not totally private and confidential and that sensitive or confidential information should be transmitted by more secure means.

Since your company's electronic media, equipment, and services should be used by your employees efficiently and economically and not in a way that is likely to cause network congestion or hamper the ability of other people to access and use your company's computer systems, any software designed to destroy data, provide unauthorized access to your company's computer systems, or disrupt computing processes should be prohibited.

To maintain the integrity of your company's confidential and proprietary information, your code of conduct should set forth specific rules for avoiding intended or inadvertent disclosure of any confidential or proprietary company information.

Your employees need to understand that messages or information sent by them to other individuals via an electronic network (bulletin board, online service, or Internet, for example) are statements identifiable and attributable to your company. While some users include personal "disclaimers" in electronic messages, it should be noted that there is still a connection with your company, and the statement might still be legally imputed to it. As a result, your company's employees should be prohibited from posting or otherwise contributing company-related information to Internet message or bulletin boards.

To ensure your company's continuous access to information on its computer systems, no company employee should be allowed to use personal hardware or software to encrypt email, voicemail, or other data stored in or communicated by your computer systems, except in accordance with express prior written permission from company management. If an employee needs to use security measures to encrypt email, voicemail, or any other data stored in or communicated by your company's computer systems, he or she should contact the appropriate information systems personnel for assistance in the encryption.

Additionally, your company's code of conduct should provide that all of its computers should be scanned regularly using current versions of its standard antivirus software. Your code should specify that before your employees use or access software designated as shareware, freeware, or public-domain, the product copyright must be reviewed by, and approval obtained from, a designated company official. Your code should require that your employees immediately report any actual or suspected misuse of your company's computers or information systems to a designated company official.

Use of Company Resources for Outside Organizations

Your company's code of conduct should allow an employee who has been requested by your company to participate in a nonprofit professional, industry, educational, civic, or charitable activity or organization (such as United Way) to use your company's property and resources to carry out the participation if the use is approved by an appropriate designated company official.

Your company's corporate code should generally prohibit your employees from using your company's resources and facilities for political purposes. This topic is addressed in more detail in Chapter 13.

Company Chatrooms

While your company should not attempt to strictly prohibit your employees from participating in any Internet message board or "chatroom" dedicated to your company, your code of conduct should prohibit your employees from disclosing any confidential, proprietary, or sensitive information about your company, your business, prospects or other employees in the chatroom. Similarly, your code should prohibit your employees from disparaging or criticizing your company, your business, your customers or suppliers, or your officers and other employees in such a chatroom.

Company Travel Resources

Your code should instruct your employees who travel on company business to use their best efforts minimize your company's travel expenses. Company business travel should be conducted in a prudent and cost-effective manner in compliance with your company's business travel policies and procedures. For example, many companies prohibit first-class airplane travel, stays at luxury hotels, meals at gourmet restaurants, and the like.

Many companies also address in their codes of conduct the treatment of business travel and lodging rewards earned by employees while on business-related travel, such as "frequent flyer" program benefits earned through hotels, car rental companies, and airline travel. In some cases, such awards are deemed to be the company's property to be used to defray future company-related business travel costs. In most cases, however, the awards an employee "earns" for business-related travel or lodging are allowed to be personally retained by the employee in recognition of the personal difficulties and inconveniences of business travel. However, your company's code of conduct may desire to prohibit the prospect of earning such personal benefits from influencing your employees' vendor selection or class of service.

Your company may also want to consider addressing in your code of conduct whether or not your employees may personally retain any compensation or rewards provided to them for delayed or denied airplane boarding. Some companies allow their employees to retain such compensation only if the delay in travel does not result in any interruption to their work schedule or additional costs to the company. Typically, codes of conduct provide that additional lodging, meals, and other expenses caused by voluntarily denied boarding are personal employee expenses that are not reimbursed by the company.

Responsibility for Safeguarding Confidential Information

Complete confidentiality of your company's proprietary or confidential business information, processes, and trade secrets must be respected and strictly maintained by your employees at all times. Employees and representatives of your company should be prohibited by your code of conduct from disclosing to third parties any non-public information involving your company or any other company doing business with you. Your employees should not be allowed to reveal to the public any information regarding decisions, plans, customers, suppliers, or competitors of your company, except by employees specifically authorized to do so by an appropriately designated official.

Your company's code of conduct should make it clear that no material information concerning your company or any other company that is not public knowledge should be used by your employees for the purpose of his or her personal gain, whether through stock transactions, real estate dealings, contracting, or any other means, nor may this information be transmitted to an individual outside of your company for your employee's personal gain.

If your company is publicly traded, your code should prohibit your employees from engaging in insider trading or in the short selling of your company's stock (that is, selling company stock that your employee does not own in a transaction from which your employee would benefit if the value of the stock declined).

More information on this topic is set forth in Chapter 10.

Access to Confidential Information

Your company's code of conduct should prohibit your employees from attempting to access or possess any of your company's confidential and proprietary information, processes, and trade secrets to which they are not authorized or entitled in the course of their work. No identification issued to your employees (including, without limitation, computer passwords, computer identification numbers, and access badges) should be allowed to be given or divulged by them to any other person, except as required in their performance of your company's business. Your company's code of conduct should not allow your employees to use or possess any company identification other than the identification specifically issued to them, unless required for your company's business.

Your company's code should not allow your employees to copy or use, except for your company's business, any computer programs, whether purchased from an outside vendor or developed by your company's employees or contract personnel. Copying of programs should be permitted only where authorized for the purpose of backup and recovery as part of normal operating procedures. Your company's code should provide that no software program purchased by your company from a vendor should be used other than in accordance with the terms of any governing license or rental agreement.

Rights to Inventions, Discoveries, and Ideas

All inventions, discoveries, and ideas relating to your company's business or products that your company's employees may make, develop, or have during their employment by your company, should be required by your company's code of conduct to be promptly and fully disclosed by your employees to an appropriate company official and should be your company's exclusive property. Your employees should be required by your code to sign all documents necessary or helpful to transfer any and all patent rights, copyrights, or title to your company with respect to any such inventions, discoveries, or ideas developed or created by your employees. This should not include inventions, discoveries, or ideas that predate your employee's service with your company.

Alcohol, Drugs, and Weapons

Your company's code of conduct should express its commitment to providing your employees with a safe and healthy work environment. Drug and alcohol abuse result in injury to the user and higher costs to your company in terms of absenteeism, theft, loss of productivity, health care costs, workers' compensation costs, and accidents. Your company's code of conduct should prohibit your employees from engaging in any of the following activities:

- Reporting to work or performing work while under the influence of alcohol, illegal drugs, or controlled substances

- Using or possessing illegal drugs or controlled substances on your company's property during working hours (including breaks and meals) or on company business

- Using alcohol on your company's property during working hours (including breaks and meals) or on company business, except in authorized situations

- Operating a company-owned or -leased vehicle while under the influence of alcohol, illegal drugs, or controlled substances

- Possessing or transporting alcohol, illegal drugs, or controlled substances in a company-owned or -leased vehicle

Illegal drugs and controlled substances should be defined broadly by your code of conduct as including all forms of depressants, hallucinogens, narcotics, stimulants, and other drugs whose use, possession, or transfer is restricted or prohibited by law.

Your company's code of conduct should make it clear that your employees, agents, and guests are not allowed possession of firearms and other weapons when they are on your company's property or engaged in company business.

Inspections and Searches

To ensure the safety of your company's employees, your company's code of conduct should provide that your employees and other persons on your company's property may be subject, in certain approved circumstances, to inspection or search of their personal property (including lockers, baggage, desks, parcels, computers, and automobiles) while on your company's property. Your code may provide that an employee who refuses an inspection or search request by authorized company personnel may be subject to discipline, including discharge.

Selling Personal Products at Work

Selling products at work for personal gain should generally not be allowed under your company's code. Items such as cosmetics, vitamins, personal care products, plastic containers, or food items should not be sold by your employees at work. However, your company's code may allow the occasional sale of products for charitable and educational organizations, such as cookies, candies, gift wrap, pizzas, raffle tickets, and so on. In these cases, however, purchases should be strictly voluntary; no employee should feel pressured to purchase a product, particularly if it is being sold by his or her superior.

Public Presentations

An employee of your company may have an opportunity to make an outside oral or written presentation on a subject relating to his or her work activities for your company, for which a fee or other compensation may be offered. Your company's code of conduct should require your employee to obtain advance review and approval of any such an opportunity by a designated company official before the presentation is made or compensation is received. Your code should also address whether or not the compensation earned by your employee for such a presentation should be remitted to the company.

Seeking Public Office

An employee may wish to participate in the political process on his or her own time and using his or her own funds, such as by running for or being appointed to public office (for example, for membership on the local planning board). Seeking public office could trigger applicable campaign finance laws governing corporate contributions; holding an office could involve the employee in the determination of issues in which your company may have an interest, such as reviewing the company's application for a permit. Accordingly, any such activity by an employee should be part of the company's code governing political activity, and employees should follow the procedures established by the policy. The policy must be applied equally to all company employees.

More information on this topic is set forth in Chapter 13.

Disclosure of Personnel Records; Employment References

Your company's code of conduct should provide that only authorized employees with valid, work-related reasons may have access to your company's personnel files. Only employment-related information should be maintained in your company's personnel files. Your code should reflect your company's policy to keep matters relating to employment or employment termination strictly confidential. All outside inquiries should be directed to the company's appropriate designated official.

7

ETHICAL TREATMENT
OF YOUR COMPETITORS

Your corporate code should make it clear that your company is committed to competing vigorously for business, fairly and honestly, based solely on the competitive merits of its products and services. Your code should prohibit your employees from taking actions to limit competition with your company. Specifically, your code should prohibit your employees from colluding or working together with your company's competitors to make agreements on pricing, rates, trade practices, costs, territories, or customers.

Chapter 11 contains additional suggested antitrust law compliance requirements that should be incorporated into your company's code of conduct.

Your code of conduct should also prohibit your employees from improperly obtaining confidential or trade secret information of your company's competitors. The Economic Espionage Act of 1996 makes these types of activity criminally illegal. Additional information on this topic is set forth in Chapter 10.

Your code of conduct should also prohibit your employees from spreading disparaging or malicious gossip about the products, services, or employees of any of your company's competitors. "Do unto others as you would have them do unto you" is a good proverb to live by in this regard.

If your company does engage in any comparison of your company's products or services against those of your competitors, your code of conduct should require that the comparisons be fair. Since comparative advertising is also subject to regulation, your code of conduct generally should require such advertising to be cleared with your company's lawyers beforehand.

8

ETHICAL TREATMENT
OF YOUR FELLOW EMPLOYEES

General Principles

Your company's corporate code of conduct should emphasize your commitment to treating all of your employees fairly and equally in all situations and to maintaining employment practices based on equal opportunity for all employees. Your code should stress your organizational respect for all employees' privacy and the treatment of all employees with dignity and respect regardless of race, color, religion, sex, national origin, age, veteran status, disability, or any other basis protected by federal, state, or local laws where your company operates. Additionally, your code should reflect your company's commitment to providing safe and healthy working conditions and an atmosphere of open communication for all your employees.

Equal Opportunity; No Harassment or Discrimination

Your company should be committed to providing a work environment that values diversity among your employees. All of your company's human resources and employment practices, policies, and activities should be focused on creating a respectful workplace in which every individual employee has the opportunity to reach his or her highest individual job potential.

Consistent with your company's obligations under the applicable federal, state, and local laws and regulations governing employment matters, your company's code of conduct should ensure that employment opportunities are provided equitably to all individuals throughout your company regardless of race, color, religion, sex, national origin, age, veteran status, disability, or any other basis protected by federal, state, or local laws where your company operates.

Your company's code should expressly prohibit any harassment or discrimination of any kind, regardless of whether the harasser or the victim is a supervisor, co-worker, supplier, customer, agent, or guest of your company. Your code should emphasize that harassment on the basis of race, color, religion, sex, national origin, age, veteran status, disability, or any other basis protected by federal, state, or local laws where your company operates is against the law and against your company's policies. Harassment may occur when the words, actions, or behavior of any of your company's employees creates an intimidating, hostile, or offensive environment. Harassment may take many forms, from overt advances to demeaning comments, jokes, language, and gestures. Such behavior may be perceived as harassment, even if it's not intended that way. Moreover, your corporate code of conduct should make it clear that unwelcome sexual advances or other inappropriate personal contact or conduct is prohibited.

Your code should provide that your company's equal employment, anti-harassment, and anti-discrimination policies and practices apply to both new job applicants and current employees and in all phases of employment at your company, including recruiting, hiring, placement, training and development, transfer, promotion, demotion, performance reviews, compensation and benefits, and separation from employment. Your code should make it clear that any violation of these policies and practices will result in appropriate disciplinary action, potentially including employment termination.

Your company's code should be designed to help your company better implement your equal employment opportunity objectives. All levels of supervision should be responsible for monitoring and complying with your company's policies and procedures for handling employee complaints concerning harassment or other forms of unlawful discrimination. Because employment-related laws are complex and vary by location, your code should require your supervisors to get the advice of your company's lawyer in advance when there is any doubt as to the lawfulness or appropriateness of proposed actions or inactions involving employment-related matters. Because of the particularly sensitive nature of this type of behavior and the potential for company and management liability and embarrassment, your company should undertake, as a top priority, employee training and education courses on identifying and avoiding harassment and discrimination.

Your code should promote a diverse and respectful workplace and create the expectation that your employees will conduct themselves in a professional and courteous manner appropriate for your company's work environment. Your employees should understand that they must be sensitive to and respectful of the concerns, values, and preferences of their fellow employees. Your code should further encourage your employees to report any inappropriate employment-related practices or actions to your company's human resources manager, general counsel, or other appropriate company official.

Your company's code should provide that all relationships among your company's employees should be appropriate for a business setting. In particular, personal relationships between a supervisor and a subordinate should be conducted so that the conduct of your employees involved is beyond reproach. The lending, giving, and advancing of money between a supervisor and his or her subordinates should be expressly prohibited by your company's code of conduct, as should be the exchange of gifts, goods, or services, other than gifts of a nominal value for seasonal or commemorative purposes.

Romantic or serious social relationships between a supervisor and a subordinate should be prohibited, or at least strongly discouraged, by your company's code of conduct. These circumstances present significant conflict-of-interest issues and a high possibility of undesirable ramifications for both of your employees involved, as well as for your company. In these circumstances, your company may consider requiring the written mutual consent of both individuals to such a romantic relationship and a waiver of rights against the supervisor and the company to later claim sexual harassment or discrimination. This consent, however, will not effectively address the perceived conflict of interests and the appearance of partiality and favoritism created by such a relationship.

Many companies have expanded their corporate codes of conduct to expressly promote employees' respect and tolerance of differences, including sexual orientation. In instances at Kodak, AT&T, and Verizon, some employees have objected to corporate gay tolerance positions on religious grounds. These situations have created difficult dilemmas for companies trying to respect the conflicting personal and religious beliefs of their various employees.

Your company's code of conduct rules on these matters should be in addition to those more specifically set forth in your company's separate policies and practices regarding sexual harassment, discrimination, and equal opportunity.

Outside Associations and Activities

Your company's code of conduct should strongly encourage participation by your employees in civic, welfare, political, and similar activities in the interest of service to your company's communities and the social and civic development of your employees. In an obviously controversial or sensitive situation, however, your code should require that your employees seek the guidance of your company's ethics compliance officer before making commitments that may prove harmful or embarrassing to your company's business interests or reputation.

In relationships your employees have with outside organizations, where the nature of the relationship is such that your company's name may be publicly identified with the outside organization, your company's code of conduct should require that your employees be more than normally sensitive to any embarrassment or negative effect that might befall your company as a result of such an association.

Additional information about this subject is included in Chapter 6.

Political Contributions

Corporate political contributions are prohibited by federal law and the laws of 23 states. Accordingly, your company's code of conduct should include provisions that outline your company's legal responsibilities regarding political contributions pursuant to the laws applicable to your jurisdictions. With respect to federal candidates (presidential, U.S. Senate, and U.S. House of Representatives), and in those states where corporate contributions are forbidden, your company policy should preclude employees and executives from making any direct corporate political contributions and prohibit the use of any company resources for political purposes that could be construed as an illegal in-kind corporate political contribution. Making contributions in the name of another is generally prohibited by federal law and the laws of most states, and it should be the policy of your company not to reimburse, directly or indirectly, any employee, attorney, agent, or third party for any political contributions made by that individual.

Additional information about this subject is included in Chapter 13.

Alcohol, Drugs, and Weapons

Alcohol or drugs can impair your employees' ability to think clearly and function effectively. Alcohol and drugs can make your company's employees less productive and endanger both the user and those around them, including other employees, as well as your company's customers, suppliers, and guests. Your company's code of conduct should strictly prohibit the use, sale, distribution, manufacture, or possession of any illegal drugs or any alcohol on your company's property. (In limited circumstances, your company may allow alcohol to be consumed on the company's premises in connection with company-sanctioned social events.) Your employees should also be prohibited from being on company property, performing any company business, or operating any company-owned vehicles or equipment while under the influence of either drugs or alcohol. Similarly, your company's code should prohibit employees' abuse of prescription drugs while on the job or company premises.

In the interests of creating a safe work environment, your code of conduct should prohibit the use or possession by your company's employees of any firearms or other weapons on your company's property or while engaged in any company business. Your code should prohibit weapons in your employees' possession even in your company's parking lots, parking garages, and company vehicles.

Abusive Language

Your company's code of conduct should encourage your employees to treat and interact with each other professionally and civilly at all times. Abusive or profane language, physical violence, and threats of physical violence should be prohibited by your code.

Employment of Relatives

Your company's code should prohibit or restrict the hiring of employees' relatives in situations where one relative would be in the line of supervision of the other, without the pre-approval of an appropriate designated company official. Your code should not allow relatives of an employee to be employed in situations that may impair your company's accounting or internal control system of checks and balances.

9

ETHICAL TREATMENT OF YOUR COMMUNITY

General Principles

Your corporate code of conduct should emphasize your company's commitment to being a responsible corporate citizen of the communities in which your business operates and to making your communities better places to live. Your company's code should not only evidence your company's commitment to abide by all national, state, and local laws, but it should also stress to your employees your company's focus on improving the well-being of the cities and towns in which your company operates. This emphasis can be reinforced through the encouragement of employee participation in civic affairs and corporate philanthropy.

Your company's code of conduct should encourage the protection of people and the environment as part of your company's overall philosophy of business conduct. Your code should promote your employees' understanding that they have the responsibility of ensuring your products and operations meet applicable government and company standards for safety. In this regard, your code should promote the elimination of all injuries, the prevention of adverse environmental and health impacts, the reduction of wastes and emissions, and the promotion of resource conservation at every stage of the life cycle of your company's products and services.

Your code should require your employees to be alert to environmental and safety issues and be familiar with environmental, health, and safety laws and your company's policies applicable to your areas of business. Since environmental, health, and safety laws are complex, are subject to frequent changes, and vary by location, your code should encourage your employees to obtain the advice of your company's lawyer when there is any doubt as to the lawfulness of any actions or inactions.

Environment

Your company's commitment to maintaining and enhancing the environment should be an important part of your company's code of conduct. Your company's code should emphasize your corporate commitment to investing in, producing, and promoting products and services that do not harm the environment. Your code should specify appropriate business practices to be followed by your employees to preserve the environment to the maximum extent reasonably possible.

Of course, your company's code should make it clear that your employees must comply with all applicable environmental laws, regulations, rules, and policies. Specifically, this should include the responsibility of your company and its employees to comply with the terms of all environmental permits required to operate your business and to provide truthful and accurate information to government permitting authorities in connection with any application you make for environmental permits or any periodic reports that those permits might call for.

Your company's code should also express its commitment to conducting your business operations in such a way as to avoid or minimize any possible adverse impact on the environment. Depending on the nature of your company's business, your code may include specific pollution prevention programs, recycling activities, waste reduction processes, energy saving programs, and water and air quality programs.

Product Safety

Your code of conduct should stress your company's commitment to selling products and services that are safe for your customers, consumers, and the public in general.

Work Safety

Your company's code should evidence your corporate commitment to creating and maintaining a safe and healthy working environment. Employees of your company should understand their responsibility to comply with all applicable laws and regulations regarding the safe design, construction, maintenance, and operation of your company's facilities and operations. Your code should make it the responsibility of every employee to perform his or her work and to conduct your company's operations in a safe manner. Your employees should be aware that health and safety laws may provide for significant civil and criminal penalties against individuals and your company for failure to comply with applicable requirements. Accordingly, your company's employees must understand their obligations to comply with all applicable safety and health laws, rules, and regulations, including occupational safety and health standards.

Community Support

Your company's code of conduct should exhibit its support of the communities in which your business operates. This civic and philanthropic support may include your company's support of local economies, housing, and educational institutions, and individuals who are economically or socially challenged or disadvantaged.

10

YOUR ETHICAL OBLIGATIONS
OF CONFIDENTIALITY

General Principles

Your company's proprietary information, processes, practices, and rights are likely to be critical to your ongoing success. Your code of conduct should specifically address your employees' obligations both to safeguard the confidentiality of your proprietary and sensitive business information and to refrain from the improper use of the proprietary and sensitive business information of your customers, suppliers, and competitors. Your company's code of conduct should also address the protection of your intellectual property rights in general, such as patents, trademarks, copyrights, and trade secrets.

Your code should also make it clear that new employees should not bring confidential information from their previous employers to their jobs with your company.

Generally, confidential or proprietary information of your company and others includes any information that is not generally disclosed, that is useful or helpful to your company, or that would be useful or helpful to competitors of your company. Common examples include such things as strategic plans, financial data, acquisition prospects, sales figures for individual products or groups of products, planned new products or planned advertising programs, areas where your company intends to expand, ways in which your company manufactures your products, product designs, lists of suppliers, lists of customers, wage and salary data, personnel data, capital investment plans, projected earnings, changes in management or policies of your company, testing data, manufacturing methods, suppliers' prices to your company, plans your company may have for improving any of your products or services, and other trade secrets.

Safeguarding Your Company's Business Secrets and Intellectual Property

Your company's code of conduct should not allow your employees to disclose or use any of your proprietary or sensitive business information, secrets, processes, or practices, except as required in their duties or with the written consent of an appropriate designated company official. Similarly, your code should not allow your employees to use or store any of your company's proprietary or sensitive business information where unauthorized personnel can see it, whether at work, at home, in public places or elsewhere. Your code should recognize that home computers, use of the Internet, social situations, and air travel require particular caution. Depending on your company's business, your code should stress that only authorized individuals who have a "need to know" should be allowed access to, and the use of, your company's proprietary or sensitive business information.

Your company's code of conduct should set forth the following guidelines on protecting your company's proprietary and sensitive business information, secrets, processes, and practices:

- Any proprietary or sensitive business information of your company should be discussed with other employees or agents of your company only on an authorized, need-to-know basis.

- If a company employee wants to disclose confidential or sensitive business information, secrets, processes, or practices of your company to people outside of your company, it should be done only in conjunction with obtaining an appropriate confidential information nondisclosure agreement, which can be provided by your company's lawyers.

- Your company's employees should avoid inadvertent disclosures that may arise either in social conversations or in normal business relations with your company's suppliers, customers, and others.

Safeguarding Others' Business Secrets and Intellectual Property

Some of your employees may become familiar or entrusted with suppliers' or customers' proprietary designs, processes, or techniques, or gain other confidential information or trade secrets of your company's suppliers or customers. Your company's code of conduct should require your employees to respect the proprietary and confidential nature of this information and not use it without authorization or otherwise disclose it to third parties.

Your code should require that your employees also respect the obligations of confidence that they may have from prior employment. Your code should provide that any company employee or contractor who, because of prior employment, is aware of another company's proprietary information or trade secrets, must not be asked to reveal these confidences or use them to your company's advantage or the prior employer's disadvantage. In this regard, your code should specify that your company's employees or contractors should not be assigned to work in a job that would require the use of a prior employer's proprietary information or trade secrets. Your code should also require that an employee immediately inform his or her supervisor if any employment at your company might cause them to violate previous obligations of confidence.

Can't Use Your Company's Confidential Information for Personal Gain

It is illegal and should be against your company's code for any individual to personally profit from undisclosed information relating to your company or any company with which you do business.

Software of Others

If your company uses software that was created and copyrighted by another company, it is likely subject to nondisclosure restrictions or a license agreement, or both. Your code should require your employees to comply with restrictions and agreements that govern the use of software. Reproducing software without authorization may violate these agreements and copyright laws. Your code should not allow your employees to copy, resell, or transfer software created by another company unless it is authorized under the applicable software license agreement.

No Insider Trading or Short Selling

Your company's code of conduct should expressly prohibit your employees from trading in the stock or other securities of your company, or those of any company that deals with it, when, as a result of their employment, they have "material nonpublic" information about your company or that firm. This restriction on "insider trading" should not be limited to trading in your company's stock or bonds. It should include trading in the securities of other firms, particularly those that are current or prospective customers or suppliers of your company and those with which your company may currently be negotiating.

In addition, your code should prohibit your employees from disclosing material nonpublic information learned or developed through their employment with your company to other persons ("tipping") who may misuse the information, and from recommending that anyone purchase or sell any securities on the basis of such information. Your code should require that, as long as material information is nonpublic, your employees and members of your employees' immediate families and others who have received the information from your employees are not permitted to trade in the securities of the company to which the information relates.

Your company's code of conduct should specify that, after material nonpublic information learned or developed through their employment has been publicly disclosed in a press release or other official announcement, your employees and their family members should not trade in the subject company's securities for 24 to 48 hours after the public announcement of the information to allow the market to absorb it and reflect it in the trading price of the security.

Under federal securities laws, insider trading and tipping can result in substantial civil and criminal penalties, including fines of up to three times the profit gained or loss avoided, and imprisonment. As the employer, your company could also be liable for fines of $1 million or more as a consequence of your employee's insider trading or tipping.

Trading by your company's employees in "puts" and "calls" (publicly traded options to sell or buy stock) of your company's stock and engaging in short sales of your company's stock are often perceived as involving insider trading or bets against your company. This type of trading is viewed by many to involve a conflict of interest, because your employee may profit from your company's stock price going down. Your company's code of conduct should therefore prohibit your employees from put and call option trading and short selling with respect to your company's securities.

In addition, to avoid even the appearance of impropriety in transactions in your company's stock, company officers and certain other designated employees should be required by your code to comply with the following restrictions:

- They must refrain entirely from trading in puts and calls in, and engaging in short sales of, your company's stock.

- They should be urged to trade in your company's stock only during company-allowed "window periods" following the date of release of a quarterly or annual statement of sales and earnings.

Additional information about this topic is contained in Chapter 11.

Improperly Obtaining Confidential Information of Others

While acquiring and having access to accurate and current market information is likely of significant interest to your company, using improper means to obtain trade secret information of others, or using such trade secret information, could expose your company or your individual employees to potentially significant civil fines or liabilities, or even criminal penalties. As a result, your company's code of conduct should prohibit your employees' use of improper means to obtain trade secret information and the use of others' trade secrets. Generally, information is considered a "trade secret" only if these three conditions exist:

- The information is in fact secret – that is, not generally known to and not readily ascertainable by the public.

- The owner has taken reasonable measures to keep the information secret.

- The information has independent economic value because it is not widely known.

In 1996, Congress passed the Economic Espionage Act, which makes it a crime to steal trade secrets. More specifically, the Economic Espionage Act prohibits your company and your employees from acquiring trade secrets of others through improper means, such as deceit or misrepresentations, and prohibits the receipt or use of information illegally acquired by a third party, or from present or former employees who are not authorized to disclose it. The Economic Espionage Act provides for criminal fines for your company of up to $10 million and criminal fines for your employees of up to $500,000 and up to 15 years' imprisonment.

11

YOUR ETHICAL OBLIGATIONS TO COMPLY WITH THE LAW

General Principles

As one of its most basic fundamental principles, your company's code of conduct should insist that your company's business be conducted by your employees in full compliance with all applicable laws, regulations, and rules. An employee's failure to obey – and ensure your company obeys – all applicable laws, regulations, and rules should be a clear and express violation of your code of conduct, since that conduct may expose not only your employee, but also your company, board of directors, and management, to criminal or civil prosecution, fine, or penalty. Your code should encourage your employees to contact your company's lawyers with questions on specific laws, regulations, and other legal issues that apply to your business.

No Bribes or Kickbacks

It should be against your company's code of conduct for your employees to pay any bribe, gratuity, or kickback, give any expensive gift, or make any similar unlawful, improper, or otherwise questionable payments to customers, suppliers, government employees, or other third parties or members of their families, in connection with the sale of any of your company's products or services. This prohibition should apply to all of your company's employees at all levels, domestic and foreign. Your code should expressly direct your employees to sell your company's products and services based solely on the merits of price, quality, service, and other competitive features. Should any such questionable payments be requested by a customer or potential customer, your code should require your employees to contact your company's lawyers or ethics compliance officer immediately.

Similarly, your company's code of conduct should prohibit your employees from accepting any business that can be obtained only by improper or illegal payments. Your company should not pay "push money" or make secret payments to employees of your company's customers or potential customers to induce them to sell your products over those of your company's competitors.

Your company's policy on prohibiting questionable payments should not stop with direct action on the part of your company's employees. Any kind of subterfuge, including payments and discounts to agents or other third parties for questionable activities of any sort, should be strictly forbidden by your code.

Moreover, your company may not close its eyes to any activity that appears to be questionable. Accordingly, your company's code should prohibit any payment being made by your company's employees to others for any purpose, other than that described in the documents supporting the expense. Your code must prohibit any false entry in your company's records, and no cash or other assets should be maintained for any purpose in any unrecorded or "off-the-books" fund.

Document Retention and Destruction

Your company's code of conduct should require the retention of certain business records for various periods of time, particularly in the litigation, tax, personnel, health and safety, environmental, contract, and corporate structure areas. In addition, when litigation or a governmental investigation or audit is pending or imminent, your code should strictly prohibit any and all relevant records (including emails) from being destroyed until the matter is closed. Destruction of records to avoid disclosure in a legal proceeding may constitute a criminal obstruction of justice offense for both your company and the employees involved.

Securities Laws

Particularly if your company is publicly traded, but even if your company issues stock to your employees or others, your company's code of conduct should evidence its commitment to fully complying with public disclosure and other requirements and rules of the applicable federal and state securities laws. Your code should require your employees to ensure that any disclosures made by your company to your shareholders, potential shareholders, or the stock market in general comply with all applicable securities laws and regulations, as well as any applicable requirements of the stock exchange or trading market on which your company's securities are traded.

In companies with publicly held securities, no employee may engage in or permit another employee to engage in any activity on your company's behalf that he or she knows, or reasonably should know, would violate securities laws. In this regard, your company's code of conduct should prohibit the following activities:

- False, misleading, or deceptive statements made in connection with the purchase or sale of a security or in any report filed with the SEC or distributed to any financial analyst or security holder
- Improper or premature disclosure of confidential information to outsiders or employees who do not need the information to perform their duties
- Trading by employees in company securities when they are aware of material information affecting your company that is not yet publicly disclosed

Antitrust

Your company's code of conduct should promote the concept that the welfare of your customers is best served by economic competition. Consequently, your company's code should reflect your commitment to competing vigorously for business and complying with the antitrust and competition laws of the jurisdictions where your company's products and services are manufactured and sold. Your company's business decisions and marketing practices should be made positively, with a view toward increasing your sales and profits, rather than negatively, with a view toward reducing some other company's sales or profits.

The antitrust laws generally prohibit practices that might unreasonably restrict competition. Your company's employees should be forbidden by your corporate code from engaging in any practices that are generally acknowledged to violate antitrust and competition laws.

Specifically, your code of conduct should prohibit your employees from agreeing with your competitors on, or discussing with your competitors, any of the following:

- Prices (including credit terms, discounts, freight rates, etc.) charged for goods or services sold – regardless of economic impact

- Terms or conditions of sale

- Levels of production

- Prices for products or services purchased

- Not competing on bids ("bid rigging")

- Not competing by allocating customers, territories, or markets

- Joining in a boycott of suppliers or customers to accomplish anti-competitive ends

- Territories in which each company will sell its products

- Customers to which each company will offer its products

- Types of products or the amount of any product that either company will produce or offer for sale in the marketplace

- Setting very low prices to drive out a competitor with the intention of raising those prices when the competitor has been driven out of the marketplace

- Exchange of competitively sensitive information (prices, terms, conditions of sale)

- Taking any other action specifically aimed at harming any individual competitor

Your company's code of conduct should also prohibit the use of "tying arrangements," where your employees condition the sale of a product on the buyer purchasing some other separate and unrelated product from your company.

Additionally, if your company uses independent distributors to market and sell your company's products or goods, then your company should consider your distributors to be independent businesses that are entitled to make all of their own business decisions. As a result, your code of conduct should generally prohibit your employees from dictating any of the following terms or conditions to your distributors:

- The price at which your distributors should sell your company's products

- The customers to whom your distributors can or cannot sell

- The territories in which your distributors can or cannot sell

Since the antitrust laws can prohibit your company from selling the same product at different prices to different customers when that price difference might have an adverse effect on competition, your company's code of conduct should require that your employees treat all similarly situated customers the same.

While your company has a clear legal right to decide to whom you will sell your products and services, this right must be exercised by your company itself and not in conjunction with other companies. Agreements between two or more companies to not do business with some third company can be a violation of the antitrust laws if the refusal to deal has an adverse effect on competition. Your code of conduct should specify that your employees should not discuss with others who your company will or will not do business with and should not attempt to persuade any other company to deny business to others.

Since your company's products and services should be sold on the basis of price, quality, service, and other competitive features, your company should be buying the products and services of others based on the same considerations. Your company's code of conduct should prohibit your employees from attempting to sell products and services to other companies on the basis of purchases made from those other companies. Similarly, your code should not allow other companies to attempt to make your company buy their products and services simply because they sell products and services to your company.

Your company's code should also prohibit your employees from setting conditions on their sale of products or services by selling to a customer only if that customer refuses to deal in the goods of one of your competitors. Similarly, your company's salespeople should not condition the sale of your products or services on your customers' refusal to deal with other suppliers.

Understanding the requirements of the antitrust and competition laws of the various jurisdictions where your company does business can sometimes be difficult. Your company's code of conduct should encourage your employees to seek the counsel of your company's lawyers about the propriety of any business practices that may involve discussions, agreements, or understandings with your company's competitors.

Environmental

Your company's code of conduct should require all of your employees to comply with all applicable federal, state, and local environmental laws. These laws are designed to protect the environment in which we live and work, human health, wildlife, and natural resources. Environmental laws either prohibit or severely restrict the release of pollutants into the air, land, surface water, and groundwater. They contain numerous waste management requirements. They impose on owners and operators of most types of facilities the duty to protect the environment by requiring them to obtain permits for certain emissions, to report release and spills of materials that may cause pollution, and to create and maintain certain records. Your company's code should have policies and operating procedures to ensure your employees strictly follow these applicable environmental laws and regulations and comply with applicable permits issued under these laws.

Product Safety Laws

Your company's code of conduct should require that all products of your company that are offered for sale meet all applicable legal safety standards.

Employment-Related Laws

Your company's employment practices and procedures must fully comply with federal, state, and local employment-related laws, including at the federal level, the Civil Rights Acts, the Age Discrimination in Employment Act, and other antidiscrimination laws, the Employee Retirement Income Security Act, the Fair Credit Reporting Act, the Fair Labor Standards Act, and the National Labor Relations Act.

Workplace Safety

Your company's code of conduct should require your employees' compliance with all applicable laws that protect health and safety. For example, the Occupational Safety and Health Act regulates both physical safety and exposure to conditions in the workplace that could harm employees. The Occupational Safety and Health Act establishes specific industrial hygiene procedures, standards for communication of precautions and hazards associated with substances your company uses or produces, and permissible exposure limits for certain substances.

Your code should require any employee who is faced with a health or safety issue to contact your company's appropriate designated official.

Political Activity

The federal law and the laws of all 50 states all contain specific and different prohibitions on various types of political activities by corporations, primarily directed toward corporate contributions to political campaigns. Your company's code of conduct should identify the jurisdictions in which your company does business and develop a corporate code of conduct for political activity based on the permissible types of activities in each.

Additionally, certain types of businesses are precluded by law from making political contributions based on the type of business in which the company is engaged. Municipal bond professionals are prohibited by rules issued by the SEC from contributing to candidates for office defined as local or state governments that issue public bonds or securities; other states prohibit corporations engaged in certain types of business from contributing to candidates for specific offices. Your company's code of conduct should incorporate not only the generally applicable law, but also any specific prohibitions applicable to the type of business or industry in which your company is engaged.

Additional information about this subject is included in Chapter 13.

Relations with Government Employees

As a general rule, your company's code of conduct should prohibit payments of money, gifts, services, entertainment, or anything of value from being offered or made available by your employees to government officials or employees. Each state and the federal government have promulgated ethics laws and regulations that specifically identify the applicable rules for business courtesies, entertaining, gifts, speaking fees, and so on, for executive and legislative officials and employees. The regulations vary by jurisdiction, but it is vital that your code incorporate the rules applicable to the jurisdictions where your company does business.

Foreign Corrupt Practices Act

The Foreign Corrupt Practices Act, in general, prohibits giving money or things of value to a foreign official for the purpose of influencing a foreign government. In general, your company's code of conduct should prohibit any such payments. The laws and regulations of foreign countries governing these matters can be quite different from those affecting the government personnel of this country.

Additional information about compliance with the Foreign Corrupt Practices Act is included in Chapter 14.

Government Requests for Information

Your company's code of conduct should require your employees to make reasonable efforts to cooperate with the departments or agencies of all federal, state, and municipal governments desiring information on the operation of your company or in connection with governmental investigations. Your code should advise your employees that if any government investigator or agency seeks information from them or access to your company's records or facilities, they should politely inform the investigator that your company's policy is generally one of cooperation, but that your employees must first obtain clearance from your company's designated official before furnishing information or access to anyone.

It should be the responsibility of your company's lawyers to represent your company in all contacts with government representatives and to determine what information is appropriate to supply to investigators. Your code should require your employees to refer governmental requests for information to your company's lawyers.

Government Investigations

Your code should require your employees to give government investigators the full measure of assistance to which they are entitled, consistent with the safeguards the law has established for the benefit of entities or persons under investigation. Your code should establish the following policies on government investigations:

- Your company's policy is to cooperate with government investigators.

- Your company's employees are required to notify your company's lawyers of any investigation of which your employees become aware.

- Your company's employees are prohibited from destroying or altering any company documents relating in any way to any governmental investigation.

- Your company's employees are prohibited from lying or making misleading statements to investigators.

- Your company's employees have the right to consult with their own legal counsel if they are questioned by an investigator.

- Your company's employees are required to forward all governmental written requests for information to your company's lawyers.

Maintenance of Books, Records, and Accounts

The financial results of your company's operations must be recorded in accordance with the requirements of law and applicable accounting principles. Your company's books, records, and accounts must, in reasonable detail, accurately and fairly reflect business transactions and dispositions of company assets. Your code should prohibit your company's employees from taking, or permitting to be taken, any action in a manner whereby your company's books, records, or accounts would not accurately, fairly, and completely reflect the action taken. No company asset or fund may be used for an unlawful purpose. No false or misleading entries are permitted, and no company asset, account, or fund may be established or acquired for any purpose unless such asset, account, or fund is accurately recorded on the company's books and records.

Additional information about this subject is contained in Chapter 12.

12

YOUR ETHICAL OBLIGATIONS TO MAINTAIN YOUR COMPANY'S FINANCIAL INTEGRITY

General Principles

Your company's accounting records should be relied upon to produce clear and accurate financial statements and reports for your company's management, board of directors, shareholders, creditors, governmental agencies, and others. Your code of conduct should clearly state your accounting, financial, and tax records, statements, and reports should be kept and presented in accordance with all applicable laws, accurately and fairly reflecting, in reasonable detail, your company's assets, liabilities, revenues, and expenses. This includes time sheets, sales records, and expense records.

Your code should require all of your company's employees to be responsible to ensure that false, artificial, or intentionally misleading entries are not made in your accounting records. Intentional misclassification of transactions as to accounts, departments, or accounting periods should be prohibited. Delaying or prepaying invoices to meet budget goals should be prohibited. Your code should also require that all commercial transactions be properly authorized, approved, and supported by accurate documentation in reasonable detail.

Your code should prohibit any cash funds, bank accounts, investments, or other assets from not being recorded or adequately recorded in your company's accounting records. Employees having information or knowledge of any unrecorded fund or asset or any other questionable financial disclosure or accounting, auditing, or financial practice or concern should be required to promptly report this to the appropriate official. If your employee is not satisfied that the issue reported has been addressed properly or does not feel comfortable raising the issue with the official, he or she should be encouraged to report the issue directly to a higher authority. If your company is publicly traded, the Sarbanes-Oxley Act requires that you adopt formal whistle-blowing processes for your company's employees to report their concerns about financial or accounting matters to your company's audit committee.

None of your company's employees should be allowed by your code have so great a span of responsibility as to make it possible for your company's internal accounting control system of checks and balances to be impaired or its assets to be diverted.

The use of any funds or other assets of, or the providing of any services by, your company for any unlawful purpose should be prohibited.

Your code should also prohibit your employees from destroying or tampering with its accounting and financial records, which should be required to be retained for a sufficient time to meet both the applicable legal requirements and those required by your company's corporate office and auditors.

Your company's code should prohibit any payment, in full or in part, from being approved or made with the intention or understanding for any purpose other than as described by the written document supporting or requiring the payment.

Your code should prohibit your employees from acting to fraudulently influence, coerce, manipulate, or mislead your company's independent auditing firm for the purpose of rendering your company's financial or tax statements misleading or inaccurate.

Senior Financial Officers/Accounting Staff

In addition to the generally applicable policies in your company's code of conduct on maintaining the integrity of your company's financial and accounting books and records, your senior financial officers (that is, your chief financial officer, principal accounting officer, controller, and other employees performing similar functions, including at the division level) should be made subject to certain additional requirements to help ensure the integrity and transparency of your company's financial, accounting, and tax statements and reports. The Sarbanes-Oxley Act requires publicly traded companies to specifically adopt provisions applicable to their senior financial officers as part of their corporate code of conduct.

If your company is publicly traded (or even if it is not), your code should make the following requirements:

- Your senior financial officers should have the responsibility to ensure the integrity, accuracy, and transparency of your company's financial statements and its compliance with all legal and regulatory requirements related to its financial statements. These officers should be required to immediately report any failures or deficiencies relating to these matters to the chairman of your company's audit committee (or a similar body or independent senior officer).

- Your senior financial officers should have the responsibility for maintaining effective internal audit functions, risk management practices and procedures, and financial reporting and compliance practices, and reporting thereon (including particularly any failures, deficiencies, or changes that could adversely affect your company's financial condition or results of operation) to your company's audit committee (or a similar body or independent senior officer).

- Your senior financial officers should have the responsibility to ensure that your company's public filings with the Securities and Exchange Commission and stock exchanges, and other reports that contain your company's financial statements, fully comply with the applicable requirements of the federal securities laws and the stock exchange on which your company's securities trade, and that the information contained in these reports fairly presents, in all material respects, the financial condition, cash flow, and results of operations of your company. These officers should be required to report any failures or deficiencies relating to these matters immediately to the chairman of your company's audit committee (or a similar body or independent senior officer).

- Your senior financial officers should have the responsibility for establishing, maintaining, and evaluating your company's internal accounting controls and for disclosing to its audit committee (or a similar body or independent senior officer) and its independent auditing firm any significant failures or deficiencies in these controls, any fraud involving employees significantly involved with them, and whether or not there were significant changes in the controls or other factors that could significantly affect them. Your code should stress that the objective of your company's internal accounting controls should be to provide assurance that all of your company's assets are adequately protected and properly used, and that its financial records accurately and clearly reflect the assets, liabilities, revenues, and expenses of your company.

- Your senior financial officers responsible for each of your company's operating divisions should be responsible for knowing what can go wrong in their areas and be alert for symptoms of loss, errors, or wrongdoing. Notwithstanding this, your company's division controllers or their equivalent should be made responsible for the overall integrity of the financial systems and controls in their divisions. They should be expected and authorized by your company's code to intervene to investigate and take action in situations within their divisions where they believe financial controls do not meet applicable standards or where the company is at risk.

- There should be no concealment of information from (or by) your senior financial officers, or from your company's internal or external auditors or legal counsel.

- No senior financial officer should be allowed to take, or allow any other employee to take, any action to fraudulently influence, coerce, manipulate, or mislead your company's independent public auditing firm for the purpose of rendering your company's financial statements materially misleading. If any of your senior financial officers becomes aware of any such circumstance, your code should require that he or she report it immediately to the chairman of your company's audit committee (or a similar body or independent senior officer).

- Your senior financial officers should have the responsibility to ensure that your company's auditing firm reports directly to its audit committee (or a similar body or independent senior officer), and that your audit committee (which should comprise only independent directors, as required by the SEC and your company's applicable stock exchange) (or a similar body or independent senior officer) is solely responsible for the appointment, compensation, and oversight of your company's independent auditing firm, including resolving any disagreements between your company's management and your auditing firm over financial disclosure or accounting or auditing policies, practices, or treatment.

85

- Your senior financial officers should have the responsibility to immediately report any employee complaints regarding financial disclosure or accounting or auditing matters, including any financial or accounting fraud (whether or not material), to the chairman of your audit committee (or a similar body or independent senior officer).

- No senior financial officer should be allowed to engage your company's auditing firm to perform audit or non-audit services without your audit committee's (or its designee's) approval (or that of a similar body or independent senior officer).

- Your senior financial officers should have the responsibility to implement procedures and practices designed to ensure that any certificates required to be signed by your company's CEO or CFO, and filed with the SEC, NYSE, AMEX, or NASDAQ, comply with all applicable requirements and otherwise support and verify the accuracy of the certifications. Your code of conduct should require your senior financial officers to report any failures or deficiencies therein immediately to your company's audit committee (or a similar body or independent senior officer).

- Your senior financial officers should have the responsibility to advise your company's audit committee (or a similar body or independent senior officer) on the areas of financial risk that could have a material adverse effect on your company's results of operation, financial condition, or cash flow and its risk assessment and risk management policies.

- Your senior financial officers should have the responsibility to ensure that your company's off-balance sheet transactions, liabilities, obligations (including contingent obligations), commitments, relationships with unconsolidated or related party entities, and derivative transactions are properly accounted for and disclosed in accordance with the requirements of the SEC, the listing standards of the NYSE, AMEX, or NASDAQ, and other applicable laws.

- Your senior financial officers should not be allowed to seek a second opinion on any significant accounting issue from an accounting or auditing firm, other than your company's independent auditing firm, without first obtaining the approval of your company's audit committee (or a similar body or independent senior officer).

- Your senior financial officers should have the responsibility to be familiar with the requirements, duties, and responsibilities imposed on them by your company's audit committee's charter and should actively and promptly comply therewith and with all requests of your company's audit committee or its designees.

13

YOUR ETHICAL OBLIGATIONS WITH RESPECT TO POLITICAL ACTIVITIES

General Principles

The influence of government at all levels has an increasingly significant impact upon business. People elected to public office help shape the laws and policies that apply to your company's business. As a result, your company and your employees have a proper interest in becoming involved in many areas of public concern.

Since laws govern the extent of corporate activity in politics, lobbying, and public policy, your code of conduct should instruct your employees with respect to these activities.

When permitted by law, your company should express your official views only through designated spokespersons on specific public issues important to your business. Such a policy cannot restrict the free speech rights of company employees to express their personal views on their own time, using their personal resources, rather than those of the company. Further, if your company does business with the government, there may be requirements for employee "whistle-blower" rights that must be incorporated into your company's code.

When permitted by law, your company may make contributions to political candidates, but only when approved by the appropriate company official or group of officials. Otherwise, your company may choose to support political candidates or party committees only through the legally permissible means of a "political action committee" established under state or federal law.

Your company's corporate funds, facilities, or other property should not be used for the support of any political candidate or political party in any jurisdiction that forbids corporate contributions, including such use for or on behalf of federal candidates. This does not mean your company cannot use corporate resources as specifically authorized by federal or state law to communicate with executives and shareholders on any subject.

When permitted by law and properly authorized by the appropriate company official, your company's corporate funds and facilities may be used to provide the needed administrative support for the operation of a political action committee or program, the purposes of which include the disbursement of financial contributions made by your employees, stockholders, and/or others to political parties or candidates.

When permitted by law and authorized by the appropriate company official, expenditures may be made by your company to inform or influence the executives and administrative employees and stockholders regarding the views of specific candidates, or to inform the voting public on a legislative or policy issue (not candidate-specific) of importance to your company's business and stockholders.

The importance of your company's knowledge of the law, incorporating the law into your company's code of conduct, and abiding by your code in actual practice, is vital. Several states and the federal law prohibit corporate contributions to any political party or candidate, including not only direct contributions but indirect use of corporate resources and facilities to support or raise funds for candidates.

However, the U.S. Supreme Court has specifically found that states cannot prohibit corporate contributions or expenditures made to influence the success or defeat of a referendum or proposition that is submitted to a public vote, such as a proposed constitutional amendment, bond issue, or tax levy. While most states require these contributions or expenditures to be publicly reported and disclosed, corporations cannot be prohibited under the U.S. Constitution from contributing to elections on issues, as opposed to candidates.

Under your company's code of conduct, both the permissible and the prohibited corporate political activities should be delineated. Political contributions or support is defined as any "thing of value" and may include such things as:

- In-kind contributions, such as use of corporate mailing lists, printing, or postage for a fundraising event for a candidate
- Purchase of ads in any publication in support of or in opposition to a candidate
- Use of your company's name or the name of any company division or subsidiary, directly or by implication, in political or campaign literature
- Use of your company's cars, aircraft, or other property by political organizations, candidates, or their staffs in connection with a political campaign
- Direct or indirect purchase of seats or tables at political dinners and fund-raisers

In jurisdictions (or issue campaigns) where corporate contributions are allowed, these corporate expenditures must nonetheless be captured and reported. In jurisdictions where such expenditures are not allowed, your company must take steps to ensure no such expenditures are made.

Furnishing employee services to any candidate or his or her staff during your employee's normal working hours should also be covered by your company's code of conduct as an expenditure of corporate resources. In the use of corporate facilities, such as allowing political candidates the same plant tour privileges as any other person, allowing candidates for political office, or others in the candidate's official campaign family, to use your company's plant facilities for campaign purposes, such as handshaking, passing out literature, group photographs with employees, or making speeches, is governed by specific laws and regulations in each jurisdiction. Your company's code of conduct should incorporate the specific provisions of state and federal law for such activities.

Since there are special legal restrictions imposed by state and federal law on the payment of an honorarium, such as for a speech, to candidates and officeholders, no such payments should be allowed to be made under your company's code of conduct without the prior approval of the appropriate official in accordance with the law applicable to the individual public official.

Your employees should be encouraged to undertake personal political activity, consistent with the interests of good citizenship, on their own time and at their own expense in support of the candidates and parties of their choice. However, your employees' political efforts must be carried out on a purely personal basis. They should not in any way imply that their actions have the concurrence or endorsement of your company. The use of corporate stationery, facilities, or work-related time in support of a candidate should be prohibited by your corporate code. Further, in no instance should your employees use their positions or titles in your company to elicit support on behalf of a candidate or political party.

Your company's corporate code of conduct should not restrict normal commercial business practices of your company or prohibit efforts by your company to provide information to legislators, regulators, and the public in the form of advertising, testimony, or properly approved communications or information releases, as well as formal lobbying activities of your company as determined by your corporate management and reflected in your corporate code of conduct. Involving company employees in communications with policy-makers is often an important avenue for promoting legislative decisions beneficial to your company. Such grassroots mobilization should be protected and promoted through your corporate code.

In countries other than the United States, the policy of your company should be determined in accordance with local law and practice.

Being Involved

Businesses and corporations too often view the world of politics and government as somewhat akin to the weather: a topic worth worrying about – but something no one can do anything about. Involvement in the political arena is then either avoided altogether or approached with apprehension or distaste.

Neither viewpoint is desirable or necessary for your company. Decision-makers at every level of government (local, state, and federal) daily wade into subject areas that affect or interfere with the ability of your company to engage in your core business of delivering services and products to your customers, creating value to your shareholders, providing jobs and income to your communities, and generating profits to your company's bottom line. For your company to avoid political awareness and involvement is to cede to strangers, opponents, and competitors gargantuan areas that directly affect your company, employees, and shareholders.

Your company should have the impact of political and public policy decisions on your company as part of your strategic plan, knowing who makes the decisions and how you can shape and influence the decision-making process for your benefit.

Your company can – and should – be involved in the political and legislative processes. Your company should take the time to become familiar and compliant with the rules of engagement for participating in this highly regulated area of law and for providing guidance to your company's employees on those matters. Your company's code of conduct should reflect this area of law and regulation.

Your company should become aware of several general areas of law, the specifics of which vary by state, federal, and local jurisdiction. Some key examples:

Lobbying and Legislative Activities

Lobbying state and federal legislatures and local government bodies is protected under the First Amendment's right to "petition the government." That right extends not only to individuals, but also to corporations. Lobbying activities are defined by federal and state law and are subject to registration, disclosure, and reporting of expenditures based on the laws of the jurisdiction in which the activities occur.

While direct lobbying activities are permissible and perfectly legal, expenditures by your company for lobbying activities are not deductible by your company as ordinary business expenses. Membership dues paid by your company to a trade association are deductible, but only up to the percentage declared by the trade association to be spent on lobbying activities by the association.

Other kinds of lobbying do not require registration or reporting, and your company's lawyer or compliance officer should be aware of the distinctions among the various types of activities designed to influence government decision-makers generally and legislators specifically.

Mobilizing company employees for specific policy communications can be a key component of success and should not be ignored or excluded from your company's code of conduct for political activities. Of course, all such mobilization efforts must be strictly voluntary on the part of the employee, and your code of conduct should provide that no repercussions or adverse employment decisions will ever be made as a result of any employee's decision not to participate.

Campaign Contributions and Fund Raising

Campaign finance rules and laws are as complex, distinct, and varied as there are jurisdictions. While federal law and 23 states prohibit corporate contributions to, or expenditures on behalf of, candidates for public office, 27 other states and the District of Columbia permit corporations to make direct contributions to their candidates. Within those states, however, restrictions vary on the sources and amounts of contributions to candidates for particular offices. For instance, Florida law permits corporate contributions to candidates for state office, but candidates for Agriculture Commissioner are prohibited from accepting contributions from a corporate entity regulated by the office, such as a corporation engaged in growing citrus products. And, while New Jersey generally permits corporate contributions to candidates, corporations engaged in or holding gambling or casino interests, as well as banking, insurance, cable television, and public utility corporations, are prohibited from contributing to state candidates. Washington state allows corporate contributions, but only from Washington state corporations.

Federal law has long prohibited corporate contributions to federal candidates and, in 2002, Congress amended the federal law to add further restrictions on corporate political activity involving federal candidates and political parties. The Bipartisan Campaign Reform Act of 2002 prohibits the national political parties from soliciting or receiving corporate contributions to the parties' non-federal accounts for party-building and support of state and local parties, often referred to as "soft money."

Direct contributions by your company to candidates are only part of the equation. Use of your company's facilities and resources to raise money for federal or state candidates in states that prohibit corporate contributions should also be prohibited by your company's code of conduct. This should include such contributions company-provided postage and printing for invitations, staff and secretarial assistance, use of customer, vendor, and other corporate mailing lists, hosting events in corporate facilities (unless specifically authorized by law), and others.

The states (and the federal laws) that prohibit corporate contributions nonetheless allow your company to establish political action committees to solicit contributions from individual corporate employees and executives that may then be used to make contributions to candidates. Your company should be familiar with the rules and regulations governing the solicitation, limits, disbursement, and reporting of contributions to and from these entities, and your company's code of conduct should reflect these requirements. Your code should also provide that legally permissible communications with company executives and stockholders will be defined by management and performed in accordance with applicable state or federal law.

Other Political Activities

State and federal law prohibits your company from interfering with the rights of your employees to vote on election day and to engage in volunteer political activities on their own time, in their own names. State laws vary, however, on whether it is permissible for your company to provide incentives to your employees to vote or mandate a minimum number of hours your employees must be allowed to be excused from work on election day to vote.

Your code of conduct regarding political activities by your employees should be equal and non-discriminatory in its application to your executives and rank-and-file employees. Your code should incorporate the laws of the jurisdictions where your employees are located. It should also address such things as providing excused absences and providing employee incentives for voting, wearing campaign buttons, displaying campaign literature or bumper stickers on company premises, and campaign activity during company time on company property. Reasonable restrictions, equally applied, are permissible and advisable, provided your company adheres to your stated policies.

Ethics Laws and Gifts to Public Officials

Your company should be mindful of the legal framework for use of corporate resources by public officials, including staff members of elected or appointed officials. Providing to government officials the use of corporate assets, such as airplanes, tickets, and facilities (such as skyboxes, conference rooms, meeting places, and hunting lodges) and hosting events for or entertaining public officials at sporting events, trips, outings, and special occasions are governed by state and federal ethics and gift laws. Your company's corporate code of conduct should incorporate the applicability of these laws and regulations to the activities in which your company engages in its interaction with public officials.

Political Activity Compliance Policy

Your company's code of conduct should set forth its standards for compliance with applicable laws and your company's policies governing political activities by your company and your employees. Your company's code should address: campaign activities, lobbying, ethics and gift rules, and voting and election-related activities, among others. Taking the time to understand the law, to establish your company's procedures and policies in accordance with the law, and to train your employees to adhere to your policies will enable your company and your employees to participate actively in the political and legislative process without fear of inadvertently violating the law.

Your company's code of conduct should articulate its policies that reflect applicable law and either regulate or prohibit your employees' actions regarding any corporate expenditure for political purposes. Whether the political candidate or committee is allowed or is not allowed to accept corporate contributions, your code of conduct should include appropriate provisions related to:

- Use of your company's property or facilities, or the time of any of your company employees, for political activity. Examples of conduct that may be prohibited include using your company's secretarial time to send invitations for political fund-raising events, using your company's telephones to make political solicitations, allowing candidates the use of your company's facilities, such as meeting rooms, for political purposes, and loaning or making available company property for use in connection with a political campaign. These are all regulated or prohibited by state and federal law and should be undertaken only in accordance with the specific provisions of your written policies that either permit or prohibit them and outline the steps an employee must follow regarding each type of activity or expenditure.

- Capturing and reporting use of corporate facilities and resources as in-kind contributions in jurisdictions where such contributions are permitted.

- Prohibiting, in all jurisdictions, the direct or indirect reimbursement of any political contribution your employees make, either through the employee's expense account or in any other way that causes the company to reimburse the employee for that contribution. This includes the cost of tickets for political fund-raising functions considered political contributions. Including the cost of any such fund-raising dinner on an expense account, even if business is discussed, is illegal in virtually every jurisdiction and should be specifically prohibited by your company's code.

Your code should emphasize that the political process has become highly regulated, and should anticipate the basic types of political activities in which employees may wish to engage. Further, your employees who have questions about what is or is not proper should consult the company's code of conduct and its designated official(s) before agreeing to do anything that could be construed as involving your company in any political activity at the federal, state, or local levels, or in any foreign country.

While your company's employees should be encouraged to, and certainly may, volunteer their services for political purposes, your code should provide that these services should be rendered on their own time and should not use company resources. It should be against your company's policy for its employees to use normal working time for political purposes not specifically authorized in the company's code, and your code should set forth specifically what is and is not permissible.

14

INTERNATIONAL BUSINESS ETHICAL CONSIDERATIONS

General Principles

While most of the principles and rules of your company's code of conduct will apply equally to all of the countries in which your company has operations, some matters do not typically arise in the United States. If your company does business internationally, a separate section of your code of conduct may need to address specific international business legal and ethical issues.

Conflicts with U.S. Laws

As an international business, your company is affected by the laws and business customs of the countries in which it operates. Your company's code of conduct should require your employees, wherever located, to be fully responsible for conducting their business activities on behalf of your company in compliance with your code and the laws of the foreign country in which they work. When your employee believes a conflict exists between your company's code and the laws of a particular foreign country, your code should require bringing the conflict to the attention of your ethics compliance officer.

In some countries, business practices may be based on codes of conduct less stringent than or different from your company's. For business dealings in these countries, your company's employees should be instructed to follow its code, unless variances permitted by applicable law and based on sound business judgment have been approved in advance by your company's ethics compliance officer or lawyers.

Foreign Corrupt Practices Act

The Foreign Corrupt Practices Act requires that your company be very careful in making payments to foreign governmental officials or agents under circumstances in which it may appear, in hindsight, that the payments were made to induce foreign officials to give your company business or buy your company's products or services. The Foreign Corrupt Practices Act prohibits the corrupt offer, payment, or gift of money or anything of value to a foreign governmental official or employee or to any foreign political candidate or party for the purpose of influencing any act or decision of a governmental body to obtain or retain business, to direct business to any person, or to secure any improper advantage. The Act also prohibits the offer, payment, or gift of money or anything of value to any third party with knowledge that all or a portion of it will be transferred to a governmental official or employee or political candidate for a prohibited purpose.

Because of the broad nature of the Act's prohibitions, it may be implicated by a wide range of activities in addition to direct bribery of a foreign official. For instance, arrangements with foreign joint venture partners, foreign agency or sponsorship arrangements, and any direct dealings with (including lavish entertainment of) foreign governmental officials or employees may raise issues under the Act.

The Act provides for stiff criminal and civil penalties. Criminal fees of up to $2,500,000 or twice the gain per offense can be imposed on your company. Violating employees may be imprisoned for up to ten years per violation and may have to pay criminal fines ranging from $1,000,000 to twice the gain from the violation. In addition, a civil penalty of $10,000 per violation may be imposed on both your company and any of your violating employees.

As a result, your company's code of conduct should clearly prohibit commercial bribery of any nature of any domestic or foreign official. Similarly, your code should require that any payments made by your employees to agents or distributors always be made strictly for services rendered, and the amount stated should be reasonable for the nature of those services.

Additionally, your company's code of conduct should incorporate the Foreign Corrupt Practices Act's requirement that your company ensure that your books and records accurately reflect the true nature of all commercial transactions represented. Your company's code should prohibit your employees from causing your books and records to be inaccurate in any way. Your code could offer such examples as:

- Making your company's records appear as though payments were made to one person when they were made to another

- Submitting expense accounts that do not reflect the true nature of the expense

- Creating any record that does not accurately reflect the true nature of the transaction

Facilitating Payments

Where it becomes necessary to expedite or secure the performance of a routine governmental action, your corporate code of conduct may allow your employees to make small payments outside the United States to foreign government officials or employees. However, your code should generally limit such payments to:

- Nominal amounts (for example, with no individual payment in excess of $250)

- Upon the initiation of a government employee

- When the government employee will not otherwise perform the routine action

The term "routine government action" includes actions ordinarily performed in, among other things, processing governmental papers (for example, visas and shipping documents), providing mail or phone services, loading or unloading cargo, scheduling inspections, and obtaining permits, licenses, or other official documents to qualify a subsidiary or affiliate to do business. The term does not include any action by a foreign government official or employee that involves a decision to award business to or continue business with your company.

Despite the foregoing, your company's code should prohibit any facilitating payment from being made to any official or employee of the United States or state government, whether the employee lives in or outside the United States.

Your corporate code should require that all such payments be identified accurately on your company's records and be properly treated for tax purposes.

Workplace Standards

As a matter of your company's fundamental business practice philosophy, your company's code of conduct may require its foreign suppliers to follow workplace standards and business practices consistent with generally accepted practices of human decency. For example, your company's code may prohibit your employees from purchasing products or services from foreign suppliers or vendors that engage in inhumane labor practices, such as using prison, forced, or child labor, using corporal punishment or other forms of mental or physical coercion, or engaging in unsafe or unhealthful working conditions.

Anti-boycott Laws

Your company's code of conduct should incorporate and explain briefly any applicable U.S. anti-boycott laws that relate to U.S. embargoes and export control laws. In general, these laws prohibit your employees from furnishing any information to certain specified countries or companies in those countries. Applicable U.S. anti-boycott laws and regulations may prohibit or severely restrict your company from participating in boycotts against countries friendly to the United States and require your company to report both legal and illegal boycott requests to the U.S. government. While these laws were passed primarily to address the Arab boycott of Israel, they apply to boycotts of any countries friendly to the United States.

Foreign Antitrust

Many foreign countries have their own antitrust laws, some of which are significantly different from U.S. antitrust law.

Your company's code of conduct should require its personnel engaged in its foreign operations to observe the antitrust and competition laws of the countries in which they operate. The European Union and virtually every European country, including many in Eastern Europe, as well as many non-European countries, now have antitrust laws that prohibit many of the same types of conduct that are prohibited under U.S. antitrust laws and, in some cases, additional types of conduct. The antitrust laws of the European Union and many other countries sometimes impose more stringent rules than exist under U.S. antitrust laws with respect to many types of business practices, including, among others: distribution agreements; patent, copyright, and trademark licenses; territorial restrictions on resellers and licensees; rebates and discounts to customers; and pricing policy in general.

Entering New Foreign Countries

Your company's decision to expand its operations into a new foreign country may result in important additional or new legal and tax implications. As a result, its code of conduct should prohibit its employees from expanding your products or services, distribution, or other operations into any new foreign country without prior consultation with your company's lawyers.

Export Controls

In general, your company's code of conduct should explain to your employees that virtually anything your company ships out of the United States must be covered by an export license. The U.S. export control laws also reach exports made by foreign affiliates of U.S. companies. In addition, many other countries have export control systems that may apply to a wide range of products. Your company's code should require your employees to fully understand, or to consult with your company's lawyer on, the applicable regulations and specific export licensing requirements that cover the export they want to make.

Imports

Your company's code of conduct should educate your employees so that they understand that all goods imported into the United States and into each foreign country in which the company is operating must pass through customs and, except in some limited cases where there are exemptions, a duty must be paid. Accurate declarations of value and sale prices of goods must be declared upon entry. Failure to do so could cause civil or criminal investigations for fraud on the customs service. These investigations may result in penalties in addition to hindering future movement of your company's goods through the ports of the country.

15

RESOURCES DIRECTORY

P: Phone   F: Fax   E: E-mail address   W: Web site address

Association for Practical and Professional Ethics
618 East Third Street
Bloomington, IN 47405-3602
P: 812.855.6450; F: 812.855.3315
E: appe@indiana.edu

Beard Center for Leadership in Ethics
A.J. Palumbo School of Business Administration
John F. Donahue Graduate School of Business
813 Rockwell Hall, Duquesne University
600 Forbes Avenue
Pittsburgh, PA 15282
P: 412.396.5475; F: 412.396.4764
W: www.bus.duq.edu

Business for Social Responsibility
609 Mission St., 2nd Floor
San Francisco, CA 94105
P: 415.537.0890; F: 415.537.0888
E: info@bsr.org; W: www.bsr.org

Canadian Centre for Ethics and Corporate Policy
360 Bloor Street West, Suite 408
Toronto, Ontario, Canada M5S 1X1
P: 416.348.8691; F: 416.348.8689
W: www.ethicscentre.com/welcome.html
W: www.businessethics.ca

The Carol and Lawrence Zicklin Center for Business Ethics Research
The Wharton School
Jon M. Huntsman Hall
Room 668, 3730 Walnut Street
Philadelphia, PA 19104-6340
P: 215.898.1166; F: 215.573.2006
W: www.zicklincenter.org

Center for Business Ethics, Bentley College
Adamian Graduate Center, Room 108
Waltham, MA 02452
P: 781.891.2981; F: 781.891.2988
E: cbeinfo@bentley.edu
W: www.ecampus.bentley.edu/resource/cbe

Ethics Officer Association
30 Church Street, Suite 331
Belmont, MA 02478
P: 617.484.9400; F: 617.484.8330
W: www.eoa.org

Ethics Resource Center
1747 Pennsylvania Avenue NW, Suite 400
Washington, DC 20006
P: 202.737.2258F: 202.737.2227
W: www.ethics.org

European Business Ethics Network
Eben Secretariat
NMH-BI
P.O. Box 4636 Sofienberg
N-0506 OSLO, Norway
P: +47.22.98.50.56; F: 47.22.98.50.02
W: www.eben.org

Institute for Business and Professional Ethics
DePaul University
DePaul Center 6000
1 East Jackson Boulevard
Chicago, IL 60604-2287
P: 312.362.6624; W: www.depaul.edu/ethics

Institute for Global Ethics
P. O. Box 563
Camden, ME 04843
P: 207.236.6658; W: www.globalethics.org

Institute of Business Ethics
12 Palace Street
London SW1E 5JA
United Kingdom
P: 44.171.931.0495; F: 44.171.821.5819

International Business Ethics Institute
W: www.business-ethics.org

North America:
International Business Ethics Institute
1725 K Street, NW, Suite 1207
Washington, DC 20006
P: 202.296.6938; F: 202.296.5897

Europe:
International Business Ethics Institute
MWB Building
10 Greycoat Place
London SW1P 1SB
P: 44.207.960.6006; F: 44.870.139.1499

International Society of Business, Economics, and Ethics
ISBEE Secretariat, Mendoza College of Business #393B
University of Notre Dame
Notre Dame, IN 46556
F: 574.631.5255; W: www.isbee.org

Maurice Young Centre for Applied Ethics
University of British Columbia
227-6356 Agricultural Road
Vancouver, BC, Canada V6T 1Z2
P: 604.822.8625; F: 604.822.8627
W: www.ethics.ubc.ca

Minnesota Center for Corporate Responsibility
1000 LaSalle Avenue, Suite 153
Minneapolis, MN 55403
P: 651.962.4120; F: 651.962.4125

Prudential Business Ethics Center at Rutgers
Rutgers Business School
111 Washington Street
Newark, NJ 07102-3027
P: 973.353.5879; F: 973.353.1273
W: www.pruethics.rutgers.edu

Society for Business Ethics
School of Business Administration
Loyola University Chicago
820 North Michigan Avenue
Chicago, IL 60611
P: 312.915.6994; F: 312.915.6988
W: www.societyforbusinessethics.org

P: Phone   F: Fax   E: E-mail address   W: Web site address

BUSINESS ETHICS TEXTS

Barry, Norman P. *Business Ethics.* Hampshire, UK: Macmillan Publishers Limited, 1998.

Boatright, John R. *Ethics and the Conduct of Business.* 3rd ed. Englewood Cliffs, N.J.: Prentice-Hall, 2000.

Bowie, Norman E. *Business Ethics.* 2nd ed. Englewood Cliffs, N.J.: Prentice-Hall, 1990.

Boylan, Michael. *Business Ethics.* 1st ed. Englewood Cliffs, N.J.: Prentice-Hall, 2002.

----. *Ethical Issues in Business.* 1st ed. Stamford, CT: Wadsworth Publishing, 1995.

Brooks, Leonard J. *Business and Professional Ethics for Accountants.* 2nd ed. Cincinnati, Ohio: South-Western Pub, 1999.

Cavanagh, Gerald S.J. *American Business Values: With International Perspectives.* 4th ed. Englewood Cliffs, N.J.: Prentice-Hall, 1998.

Cavanagh, Gerald F., and Arthur F. McGovern. *Ethical Dilemmas in the Modern Corporation.* 1st ed. Englewood Cliffs, N.J.: Prentice-Hall, 1988.

Chakraborty, S.K. *Values and Ethics for Organizations: Theory and Practices.* Oxford, UK: Oxford University Press, 1999.

Davies, Peter, and John Quinn. *Ethics and Empowerment.* Hampshire, UK: Macmillan Publishers Limited, 1999.

De George, Richard T. *Business Ethics.* 5th ed. Englewood Cliffs, N.J.: Prentice-Hall, 1999.

DesJardins, Joseph R., and John J. McCall. *Contemporary Issues in Business Ethics.* 4th ed. Stamford, CT: Wadsworth Publishing, 2000.

Dienhart, John W. *Business, Institutions, and Ethics: A Text with Cases and Readings.* Oxford, UK: Oxford University Press, 1999.

Donaldson, Thomas. *The Ethics of International Business.* Oxford, UK: Oxford University Press, 1990.

Donaldson, Thomas, and Patricia H. Werhane, eds. *Ethical Issues in Business.* 2nd ed. Englewood Cliffs, N.J.: Prentice-Hall, 1983.

Fort, Timothy L. *Ethics and Governance: Business as Mediating Institution.* Oxford, UK: Oxford University Press, 2001.

French, Peter. *Corporate Ethics.* Stamford, CT: Wadsworth Publishing, 1995.

French, Warren, and John Granrose. *Practical Business Ethics.* 1st ed. Englewood Cliffs, N.J.: Prentice Hall, 1995.

Gilbert, Daniel R. *Ethics Through Corporate Strategy.* Oxford, UK: Oxford University Press, 1997.

Green, Ronald M. *The Ethical Manager: A New Method for Business Ethics.* 1st ed. Englewood Cliffs, N.J.: Prentice-Hall, 1994.

Hartman, Edwin M. *Organizational Ethics and the Good Life.* Oxford, UK: Oxford University Press, 1997.

Lawrence, Anne, James Post, and James Weber. *Business & Society: Corporate Strategy, Public Policy, and Ethics with PowerWeb.* New York, N.Y.: McGraw-Hill/Irwin, 2001.

Maidment, Frederick, and William Eldridge. *Business in Government and Society: Ethical, International Decision-Making.* 1st ed. Englewood Cliffs, N.J.: Prentice Hall, 2000.

Parkinson, J. E. *Corporate Power and Responsibility: Issues in the Theory of Company Law.* Oxford, UK: Oxford University Press, 1995.

Roussouw, Deon. *Business Ethics.* 2nd ed. Oxford, UK: Oxford University Press, 2002.

Shaw, William H. *Business Ethics.* 4th ed. Stamford, CT: Wadsworth Publishing, 2002.

Shaw, William H., and Vincent Barry. *Moral Issues in Business.* Stamford, CT: Wadsworth Publishing, 2001.

Solomon, Robert C. *A Better Way to Think About Business: How Values Become Virtues.* Oxford, UK: Oxford University Press, 1999.

Solomon, Robert C. *Above The Bottom Line.* 2nd ed. Stamford, CT: Wadsworth Publishing, 1994.

Steward, David. *Business Ethics.* New York: McGraw-Hill, 1995.

Sternberg, Elaine. *Just Business: Business Ethics in Action.* Oxford, UK: Oxford University Press, 2000.

Trevino, Linda Klebe, and Katherine A. Nelson. *Managing Business Ethics: Straight Talk About How to Do it Right.* 2nd ed. New York: John Wiley, 1999.

Vallance, Elizabeth. *Business Ethics at Work.* Cambridge, UK: Cambridge University Press, 1995.

Velasquez, Manuel G. *Business Ethics: Concepts and Cases.* Englewood Cliffs, N.J.: Prentice-Hall, 2002.

APPENDIX

EXAMPLES OF
CORPORATE CODES OF CONDUCT

The Coca-Cola Company: **the code of business conduct**

**The most valuable asset of
The Coca-Cola Company
is our trademark.
Its value has been built over
more than a century by
the commitment and integrity
of Coca-Cola employees.**

Dear Colleague:

You and I are fortunate to work for a company whose reputation is one of the most powerful and enduring in the world, in any industry, at any time in history. A reputation of this stature comes with an equally significant responsibility: keep it strong, consistent and relevant. To a large extent, our reputation determines how people think and feel about our products, how they see our work, and how we're valued as an organization and as an investment.

Our reputation is built on our promise—an unspoken bond between the public and our company. This promise sets expectations for Coca-Cola's performance in quality, the environment and in our diversity as an organization. Our promise also includes our personal and professional commitment to act in every instance with honesty, integrity, accountability and respect.

That's where you come in.

This new Code of Business Conduct is here to help all of us play by the rules, wherever we operate around the world. The Code has been simplified to provide clear, easy-to-understand principles to guide our conduct. These principles are illuminated by real-world examples of right and wrong under the Code.

The Code applies to all directors, officers and employees, no matter where you work, so it's important that you read it and understand it. Keep it with you and refer to it frequently. Ask whatever questions you may have. Together with other guidelines, such as our company's Principles of Citizenship and our Supplier Code, the Code of Business Conduct helps protect our reputation for integrity—and keep our promise as a company.

As a representative of The Coca-Cola Company, you hold our company's reputation in your hands. With your help, I am confident that our company will continue to be an outstanding corporate citizen in every community we serve, and our reputation for integrity will endure. Thank you for joining me in this effort.

Douglas N. Daft

CHAIRMAN, BOARD OF DIRECTORS, AND
CHIEF EXECUTIVE OFFICER

OUR PROMISE
The Coca-Cola Company exists to benefit and refresh everyone it touches.

YOUR COMMITMENT
As a representative of The Coca-Cola Company, *you must act with honesty and integrity in all matters.*

WHAT'S IN THIS BOOK—AND WHY IT MATTERS

The most valuable asset of The Coca-Cola Company is our trademark. Among the important things this trademark represents is our Company's reputation for honesty and integrity. That reputation endures because of our shared values and especially our commitment to conduct business in the right way.

This Code of Business Conduct is designed to give you a broad and clear understanding of the conduct expected of all our employees everywhere we do business. The Code of Business Conduct applies to all directors, officers and employees of the company and its subsidiaries, who, unless otherwise specified, will be referred to jointly as "employees."

What you will see in the pages that follow are a series of conduct and ethical guidelines, including examples of real-life dilemmas faced by company employees. Most of what you will read probably won't surprise you, for the overarching theme of these guidelines can be summed up this way: As a representative of the company, you must act with honesty and integrity in all matters.

SOME HIGHLIGHTS OF THE CODE

- Employees must follow the law wherever they are around the world.

- Employees must avoid conflicts of interest. Be aware of appearances.

- Financial records—both for internal activities and external transactions— must be timely and accurate.

- Company assets including computers, materials and work time—must not be used for personal benefit.

- Customers and suppliers must be dealt with fairly and at arm's length.

- Employees must never attempt to bribe or improperly influence a government official.

- Employees must safeguard the company's nonpublic information.

- Violations of the Code include asking other employees to violate the Code, not reporting a Code violation or failing to cooperate in a Code investigation.

- Violating the Code will result in discipline. Discipline will vary depending on the circumstances and may include, alone or in combination, a letter of reprimand, demotion, loss of merit increase, bonus or stock options, suspension or even termination.

- Under the Code, certain actions require written approval by your Principal Manager. The Principal Manager is your Division President, Group President, Corporate function head, or the General Manager of your operating unit.

- For those who are themselves Principal Managers, written approvals must come from the General Counsel and Chief Financial Officer. Written approvals for executive officers and directors must come from the Board of Directors or its designated committee.

- **If you have questions about any situation, ask. Always ask.**

This Code should help guide your conduct. But the Code cannot address every circumstance and isn't meant to; this is not a catalogue of workplace rules. You should be aware that the company has policies in such areas as fair competition, securities trading, workplace conduct and environmental protection. Employees should consult the policies of The Coca-Cola Company in specific areas as they apply.

YOUR RESPONSIBILITIES

- It is your responsibility to read and understand the Code of Business Conduct. You must comply with the Code in both letter and spirit. Ignorance of the Code will not excuse you from its requirements.

- Follow the law wherever you are and in all circumstances.

- Never engage in behavior that harms the reputation of the company. If you wouldn't want to tell your parents or your children about your action—or wouldn't want to read about it in a newspaper—don't do it.

- Some situations may seem ambiguous. Exercise caution when you hear yourself or someone else say, "Everybody does it," "Maybe just this once," "No one will ever know" or "It won't matter in the end." These are signs to stop, think through the situation and seek guidance. Most importantly, don't ignore your instincts. Ultimately, you are responsible for your actions.

- You have several options for seeking guidance. You may discuss concerns with your manager, responsible employees in the Finance or Legal Divisions or, in the case of potential criminal issues, with Strategic Security.

- Employees are obliged to report violations, and suspected violations, of the Code. This includes situations where a manager or colleague asks you to violate the Code. In all cases, there will be no reprisals for making any reports, and every effort will be made to maintain confidentiality.

- You can report violations of the Code to your manager or higher levels of management, to the Corporate Legal or Audit Departments, or to your division legal counsel. Employees in the United States also may report violations at 1-866-846-2653. In the case of potential criminal violations, contact Strategic Security at 1-800-515-2022 and company legal counsel.

- Employees are obliged to cooperate with investigations into Code violations and must always be truthful and forthcoming in the course of these investigations.

- Managers have important responsibilities under the Code. Managers must understand the Code, seek guidance when necessary and report suspected Code violations. If a manager knows that an employee is contemplating a prohibited action and does nothing, the manager will be responsible along with the employee.

- **The most important message is this: When you are uncertain about any situation, ask for guidance.**

CONFLICTS *of* INTEREST

OVERVIEW

Your personal activities and relationships must not conflict, or appear to conflict, with the interests of the company. Keep in mind, the Code can't specifically address every potential conflict, so use your conscience and common sense. When questions arise, seek guidance.

GENERAL PRINCIPLES

- Avoid situations where your personal interests conflict, or appear to conflict, with those of the company.

- You may own up to 1% of the stock in a competitor, customer or supplier without seeking prior approval from your Principal Manager so long as the stock is in a public company and you do not have discretionary authority in dealing with that company. If you want to purchase more than 1% of the stock in a customer, competitor or supplier, or the company is nonpublic or you have discretionary authority in dealing with the company, then the stock may be purchased only with prior approval of your Principal Manager.

- Directors may own the stock of suppliers, customers and competitors. However, a director must remove himself or herself from any Board activity that directly impacts the relationship between the company and any supplier, customer or competitor in which the director has a financial interest.

- If you have a financial interest in a transaction between the company and a third party— even an indirect interest through, for example, a family member—that interest must be approved by your Principal Manager prior to the transaction. However, if you have a financial interest in a supplier or customer only because someone in your family works there, then you do not need to seek prior approval unless you deal with the supplier or customer or your family member deals with the company.

- For any transaction that would require reporting under SEC rules, directors of The Coca-Cola Company must obtain written confirmation from the Board of Directors or its designated committee that the proposed transaction is fair to the company.

- If you'd like to serve as an officer or director or consultant to an outside business on your own time, you must receive prior approval in writing from your Principal Manager. If your Principal Manager changes, or the circumstances of the outside business change substantially, you must seek re-approval. (Employees are permitted, however, to serve on charity boards or in family businesses that have no relationship to the company.) This rule does not apply to non-employee directors of the Company.

- Any potential conflict of interest that involves an officer of the company, of a division or of a subsidiary must be approved in advance by the General Counsel and Chief Financial Officer. Any potential conflict of interest that involves a director or executive officer of the company must be approved by the Board of Directors or its designated committee.

- Loans from the company to directors and executive officers are prohibited. Loans from the company to other officers and employees must be approved in advance by the Board of Directors or its designated committee.

THE CODE IN REAL LIFE

The action: An administrative assistant's husband owns an office supply firm with lower prices than anyone else. The assistant's duties at the company included ordering office supplies, so she ordered them from her husband's firm. But she didn't ask her Principal Manager for prior approval of the transaction with a family member.

The decision: The employee violated the Code of Business Conduct. A Principal Manager must approve in advance any transaction in which an employee has a financial interest. The employee was disciplined.

The action: An account executive considered buying stock in a regional pizza chain, which was one of his customers. He asked his manager whether it was a violation of the Code.

The decision: His manager investigated the matter and advised that it would be a violation of the Code to invest in the customer's business without Principal Manager approval. That's because the account executive had discretionary authority in dealing with that customer. It may be difficult to deal with customers at arm's length when an employee has a personal financial interest.

The action: A route salesperson services a restaurant chain owned by his cousin. The salesperson wonders if that relationship requires special action.

The decision: Yes, it does require special action. All customers must be treated fairly and honestly. Even if the cousin's restaurant is not receiving preferential treatment, the relationship could give the appearance of such treatment. The salesperson should tell his

106

manager about the relationship, and the sales manager may decide to put a different salesperson on that account.

The action: A company chemist's wife is employed by a large utility that is a supplier to the company. The wife has no business dealings with the company, and the chemist has no business dealings with the utility. Is the chemist obliged to disclose the relationship?

The decision: No. But the chemist must seek his Principal Manager's approval if his job changes so that he deals with the utility, or his wife's job changes so that she deals with the company.

FINANCIAL RECORDS

OVERVIEW

Every company financial record—including time sheets, sales records and expense reports—must be accurate, timely and in accordance with the law. These records are the basis for managing the company's business and for fulfilling its obligations to share owners, employees, customers, suppliers and regulatory authorities.

If you know of violations by others, take note: You must report those instances, or you are in violation of the Code. Accurate records are everyone's responsibility. It's always a good idea to double-check them.

GENERAL PRINCIPLES

- Always record and classify transactions in the proper accounting period and in the appropriate account and department. Delaying or prepaying invoices to meet budget goals is a violation of the Code.

- Never falsify any document or distort the true nature of any transaction.

- All transactions must be supported by accurate documentation.

- All reports made to regulatory authorities must be full, fair, accurate, timely and understandable.

- Employees must cooperate with investigations into the accuracy and timeliness of financial records.

- To the extent estimates and accruals are necessary in company reports and records, they must be supported by appropriate documentation and based on good faith judgment.

- Payments can only be made to the person or the firm that actually provided the goods or services, and must be made in the supplier's home country, where it does business, or where the goods were sold or services provided, unless approved in advance by the Chief Financial Officer and General Counsel.

THE CODE IN REAL LIFE

The action: As the year was coming to a close, a plant manager realized that his operation already had exceeded the profit target in its annual business plan. The plant manager asked

Division Finance if he should hold any further income received that year off the books in order to get a head start on the next year.

The decision: "Don't even think about it!" he was told. All income and expenses must be recorded in the period they are actually realized.

The action: An employee submitted a time report for weekend overtime. Her supervisor was skeptical that she had worked the extra hours and checked weekend logs of entries into the building.

The decision: Put on notice that there was no record of her being in the building, the employee confessed to falsifying her time report. She was disciplined.

The action: Two employees on a business trip ate dinner at a restaurant. One of them paid for the meal and was reimbursed by the company for the expense. The other employee took a duplicate receipt and submitted an expense report for money he didn't spend.

The decision: The second employee was fired. He didn't pay for the meal, and so was stealing from the company.

The action: A plant manager asked some suppliers to delay sending invoices until the following year for goods already received. He did this to stay within his annual budget.

The decision: A plant employee knew of the request and that it was a Code violation. The employee reported it to a company attorney. That was the right thing to do. The plant employee also could have reported it to division management or the Corporate Audit Department.

The action: A customer demanded that a salesperson alter an invoice. The customer wanted the invoice to show a higher price than he actually paid and delivery to a different country than was actually the case. The customer asserted that he would no longer buy from the company unless the salesperson agreed to the falsified invoice.

The decision: The salesperson knew that the demand was a violation of the Code and refused to play along with the customer. The salesperson then informed his supervisor of the circumstances. That was the right thing to do.

USE *of* COMPANY ASSETS

OVERVIEW

Company assets are meant for company, not personal, use. Company assets include your time at work and work product, as well as the company's equipment and vehicles, computers and software, company information, and trademarks and name.

Common sense should prevail, of course. The occasional personal phone call from your workplace, for example, is inevitable. Substantial personal phone calls, however, represent misuse. The point is to recognize that theft or deliberate misuse of company assets is a violation of the Code.

GENERAL PRINCIPLES

- You may not use the company's assets for your personal benefit or the benefit of anyone other than the company.

- You may not take for yourself any opportunity for financial gain that you find out about because of your position at the company or through the use of company property or information.

- Misuse of company assets may be considered theft and result in termination or criminal prosecution.

- You must have permission from your Principal Manager before you use any company asset—including information, work product or trademark—outside of your company responsibilities.

- Before accepting payment for speeches or presentations related to the company or your work at the company, always get your Principal Manager's approval.

- Company computer systems and equipment are meant for company use only. For example, they should never be used for outside businesses, illegal activities, gambling or pornography.

THE CODE IN REAL LIFE

The action: A company employee's responsibilities included brand management. On his own time, he began marketing that expertise, using materials prepared as part of his work at the company and giving talks on the topic to other companies for a fee.

The decision: He never sought his Principal Manager's approval. When his outside work came to light, he was disciplined.

_____

The action: A plant operations manager used her company phone and cell phone for personal calls excessively.

The decision: It may not sound like much, but the company's losses in work time and phone charges totaled thousands of dollars. She was disciplined.

_____

The action: An administrative assistant used his computer at work on a regular basis to create party invitations and personal announcements for other employees to use. He wasn't paid for the work, so he saw no harm.

The decision: Use of the company's computers for such large-scale personal projects is a violation of the Code. The employee was disciplined.

_____

The action: An account executive had a friend who wanted to borrow a list of company e-mail addresses. The friend wanted to send e-mail solicitations for his business to company employees.

The decision: The account executive knew that would be a misuse of company assets. He explained that to his friend, and declined the request. That was the right thing to do.

The action: A manager persistently asked his administrative assistant to take care of the manager's personal business on company time, such as picking up dry cleaning, balancing his checkbook and shopping for personal gifts, and thereby consistently kept the assistant from completing her work duties.

The decision: A worker's time is a company asset. The manager was disciplined for persistent misuse of assets.

WORKING *with* CUSTOMERS & SUPPLIERS

OVERVIEW

It often is customary to exchange gifts and entertainment with customers and suppliers. The key is to keep an arm's length relationship. Avoid excessive or lavish gifts that may give the appearance of undue influence. Avoid personal financial transactions with customers and suppliers that may influence your ability to perform your job.

You should know that special restrictions apply when dealing with government employees. For more information, see the next section on Working With Governments. In all cases, when in doubt, seek guidance.

GENERAL PRINCIPLES

- The Code prohibits employees from accepting lavish gifts or entertainment. This is an area in which your judgment is critical. For instance, modest holiday gifts are usually fine. But an expensive weekend trip probably would not be. If you are uncertain, seek prior written approval from your Principal Manager.

- Gifts and entertainment for customers, potential customers and suppliers must support the legitimate business interests of the company and should be reasonable and appropriate under the circumstances. Always be sensitive to our customers' and suppliers' own rules on receiving gifts and entertainment.

- Company stock cannot be given as a gift on behalf of the company under any circumstances.

- Consistent with the obligation we all have to act with integrity and honesty at all times, you should deal fairly with the company's customers, suppliers, competitors and employees. No director, officer or employee should take unfair advantage of anyone through misrepresentation or any unfair business practice.

THE CODE IN REAL LIFE

The action: A purchasing coordinator received a diamond watch from a supplier who does a lot of business with the company. The purchasing coordinator and the supplier are friends. The purchasing coordinator graciously returned the watch, explaining that the company doesn't allow lavish gifts, and reported the incident to her supervisor.

The decision: The employee made the right call. She knew that the watch could influence her buying decisions—or that it might appear that way to others.

The action: A senior member of management sought and received a $150,000 personal loan from a company supplier.

The decision: The loan was never repaid and, after the supplier contacted company officials, the executive was fired.

The action: An account executive played in a business-related golf tournament. He won the tournament, and accepted the prize—a Caribbean cruise. He checked with his manager for approval.

The decision: Keeping the prize was fine, it was a legitimate test of skill or luck, and a large number of people participated in the tournament.

The action: A facilities manager supervised a contractor doing renovation work at the company. The contractor suggested that since he had extra time, he could do some work on the manager's home at a deep discount. The manager declined and reported the incident to her supervisor.

The decision: The employee made the correct decision. She knew that this was a favor beyond common courtesy, available only because she had hired the contractor for a company project.

WORKING *with* GOVERNMENTS

OVERVIEW

Conducting business with governments is not the same as conducting business with private parties. These transactions often are covered by special legal rules. You should consult with company legal counsel to be certain that you are aware of any such rules and you must have approval of local legal counsel before providing anything of value to a government official.

The company prohibits the payment of bribes to government officials. "Government officials" are employees of any government anywhere in the world, even low-ranking employees or employees of government-controlled entities. The term "government officials" also includes political parties and candidates for political office. It is your obligation to understand whether someone you deal with is a government official. When in doubt, consult legal counsel.

In some countries it may be customary at times to pay government employees for performing their required duties. These facilitating payments, as they are known, are small sums paid to facilitate or expedite routine, non-discretionary government actions, such as obtaining phone service or an ordinary license. In contrast, a bribe, which is never permissible, is giving or offering to give anything of value to a government official to influence a discretionary decision.

Understanding the difference between a bribe and a facilitating payment is critically important. Consult with your division legal counsel before acting.

Our company and its subsidiaries must comply with all applicable trade restrictions and boycotts imposed by the U.S. government. (A boycott is a restriction on a company's ability to ship goods into a specific country or do business there.) Moreover, our company and its subsidiaries also must abide by U.S. anti-boycott laws that prohibit companies from participating in any international boycott not sanctioned by the U.S. government. If questions arise, contact legal counsel.

GENERAL PRINCIPLES

- The ban on bribes applies to third parties acting on behalf of the company, including all contractors and consultants. Employees must not engage a contractor or consultant if the employee has reason to believe that the contractor or consultant may attempt to bribe a government official.

- The company may hire government officials or employees to perform services that have a legitimate business purpose, with the prior approval of the Principal Manager. For example, an off-duty police officer might provide security. Government officials should never be hired to perform services that conflict with their official duties.

- All facilitating payments must be approved in advance by division legal counsel and recorded appropriately.

- Employees must comply with all U.S. boycott and anti-boycott restrictions.

- The company may operate and fund through its employees one or more political action committees.

- Political contributions by the company must be in accordance with local law. They must be approved by both your Principal Manager and the General Counsel and they must be properly recorded.

- Employees will not be reimbursed for political contributions. Your job will not be affected by your choices in personal political contributions.

THE CODE IN REAL LIFE

The action: A finance manager paid $20 to an employee of a government-owned telephone company to ensure a telephone line was installed at a company office on time. Even for that small amount, she sought approval from Division Legal Counsel and recorded the transaction as a "facilitating payment."

The decision: That was smart. if the payment had been large, say $600, that might be an indication that this was not a routine governmental action and might constitute a bribe. In every case, employees must seek approval for facilitating payments, and must record these actions appropriately.

The action: An account executive was traveling in a country experiencing civil unrest. A soldier stopped him at a bridge and demanded payment.

The decision: When personal safety is at risk, the employee should, of course, make the payment. Still, the fee must be reported to the Division Legal Counsel and recorded appropriately.

The action: A general manager entertained a government official in charge of issuing special permits to allow route trucks in a restricted area. During the meeting, the general manager gave a television and DVD player to the official as "a token of respect for the esteemed minister."

The decision: That was a bribe. It was a violation of both the Code and the law.

PROTECTING INFORMATION

OVERVIEW

It is your obligation to safeguard the company's nonpublic information. You should not share this information with anyone outside the company unless it is necessary as part of your work responsibilities.

Nonpublic information is any information that has not been disclosed or made available to the general public. Trading in stocks or securities based on nonpublic information, or providing nonpublic information to others so that they may trade, is illegal and may result in prosecution.

Nonpublic information includes items such as financial or technical data, plans for acquisitions or divestitures, new products, inventions or marketing campaigns, personal information about employees, major contracts, expansion plans, financing transactions, major management changes and other corporate developments.

GENERAL PRINCIPLES

- Do not disclose nonpublic information to anyone outside the company, except when disclosure is required for business purposes and appropriate steps have been taken to prevent misuse of the information.
- Employees may not buy or sell stocks or securities based on nonpublic information obtained from their work at the company.
- Disclosing nonpublic information to others, including family and friends, is a violation of the Code and may violate the law.
- Just as the company values and protects its own nonpublic information, we respect the nonpublic information of other companies. If you have any questions about obtaining or using nonpublic information of other companies, contact company legal counsel for guidance.

113

- Records should be retained or discarded in accordance with the company's record retention policies. Consult with company legal counsel regarding retention of records in the case of actual or threatened litigation or governmental investigation.

THE CODE IN REAL LIFE

The action: A marketing manager was preparing a presentation on a new company promotion. She was excited about the plan and wanted to discuss it with a friend outside the company. She wasn't sure if that would be a Code violation, so she checked with her manager.

The decision: It's a good thing she checked. Sharing nonpublic information is a Code violation, even if the recipient doesn't work for a competitor, customer or supplier.

The action: An administrative assistant heard an office rumor that the company was considering acquiring a small, publicly traded beverage firm. She wondered if it was OK to acquire some of the stock of the other beverage company. She asked her manager.

The decision: Don't buy the stock, the manager said, after seeking advice from company legal counsel. It's a violation of the Code and a violation of securities laws on insider trading. She didn't buy the stock—it wasn't worth going to jail or losing her job.

The action: A manager was seeking a supplier to provide construction work for the company and received three sealed bids for the job. The manager gave his favorite firm the details of the competing bids so that firm could win the business.

The decision: That was wrong. The manager disclosed nonpublic company information and circumvented the bidding process. He was disciplined.

The action: A company attorney was traveling with a colleague on a plane to work on a legal case. They began to discuss the particulars of the case when one of them noticed a man across the aisle listening intently and taking notes.

The decision: They quickly decided it was time to drop the subject. It's never a good idea to discuss company matters in public where others might hear and take advantage of the information.

The action: After an important competitor held a meeting at a hotel, a hotel security guard offered a tape recording of the meeting to a company employee. The company employee wasn't sure what to do, so he took the tape to his manager.

The decision: The company employee should never have taken possession of the tape. It was wrong. No one listened to the tape, and the employee's manager promptly returned it. But even so, the competitor learned of the situation and brought a claim against the company.

ADMINISTRATION *of* THE CODE

DISTRIBUTION

All company directors, officers and employees will receive a copy of this Code at the time they join the company and will receive periodic updates. Also, any agent, consultant, government official or government employee who is retained by the company should receive this Code and understand the obligations under it.

APPROVALS

The appropriate Principal Managers must review and approve in writing any circumstance requiring special permission, as described in the Code. Copies of these approvals should be maintained by the company and made available to auditors or investigators.

Waivers of any provision of this Code for officers or directors must be approved by the Board of Directors or its designated committee and promptly will be disclosed to the extent required by law or regulation.

MONITORING COMPLIANCE

Employees should take all responsible steps to prevent a Code violation.

Employees should report suspected Code violations to their manager or higher levels of management, to the Corporate Legal or Audit Departments, or to division legal counsel. Employees in the United States also may report violations at 1-866-846-2653. In the case of potential criminal violations, employees should contact Strategic Security at 1-800-515-2022 and company legal counsel.

INVESTIGATIONS

The responsibility for administering the Code, investigating violations of the Code and determining corrective and disciplinary action rests with the General Counsel and Chief Financial Officer.

The company's Audit, Legal and Security Departments may conduct or manage investigations as deemed appropriate on behalf of the General Counsel and Chief Financial Officer. They will work together with the employee's managers to recommend corrective and disciplinary actions for presentation to the General Counsel and the Chief Financial Officer. For more information on the procedures that generally will be followed in the case of potential code violations, please refer to the Procedural Guidelines for the Code of Business Conduct. The company will follow local grievance procedures in countries where such procedures apply.

If allegations involve criminal conduct, employees should seek guidance from Strategic Security and the Legal Division before engaging in any inquiries.

The Chief Financial Officer and the General Counsel will periodically report Code violations and the corrective actions taken to the Audit Committee of the Board of Directors.

DISCIPLINARY ACTIONS

The company strives to impose discipline for each Code violation that fits the nature and particular facts of the violation. The company uses a system of progressive discipline. The company generally will issue warnings or letters of reprimand for less significant, first-time offenses. Violations of a more serious nature may result in suspension without pay, demotion, loss or reduction of bonus or option awards, or any combination. Termination of employment generally is reserved for conduct such as theft or other violations amounting to a breach of trust, or for cases where a person has engaged in multiple violations.

Violations of this Code are not the only basis for disciplinary action. The company has additional policies and procedures governing conduct.

SIGNATURE AND ACKNOWLEDGMENT

All new associates must sign an acknowledgment form confirming that they have read the Code and understand its provisions. Failure to read the Code or to sign an acknowledgment form, however, does not excuse an associate from the terms of this Code.

IT'S UP TO YOU

Administration of the Code is everyone's responsibility. There are colleagues to help you do the right thing. If you act with integrity and seek guidance when you are uncertain, you'll be doing the right thing.

This Code is not an express or implied contract of employment and does not create any contractual rights of any kind between The Coca-Cola Company and its employees. In addition, all employees should understand that this Code does not modify their employment relationship, whether at will or governed by contract.

The Coca-Cola Company reserves the rights to amend, alter or terminate this Code at any time and for any reason.

The following questions and answers set out the procedures relevant to potential violations of Business Conduct. Recognizing that no set of guidelines can cover all circumstances, these guidelines may be varied as necessary in particular cases and also may be modified to conform to local law or contract. Nevertheless, it is our intent that these guidelines be followed in most cases where a potential violation of the Code has occurred.

REPORTING

Q   To whom should an employee report suspected violations of the Code?

A   You can report violations of the Code to your manager or higher levels of management, to the Corporate Legal or Audit departments or to your division legal counsel. Employees in the United States also may report violations toll free at 1-866-846-2653. In the case of potential criminal violations, contact Strategic Security at 1-800-515-2022 and company legal counsel.

Q   Will there be any retaliation for reporting a violation of the Code?

116

A   Absolutely not. You can report suspected violations of the Code without fear of reprisal or retaliation.

Q   Can an employee report a suspected violation of the Code confidentially?

A   Every effort will be made to maintain in confidence the identity of a person making a report of a suspected Code violation.

INVESTIGATION

Q   Who should take the lead in investigating suspected Code violations?

A   The investigation normally will be conducted by the local division Finance and Legal departments. Corporate Audit must be notified of any investigation and also may be involved in the investigation, especially if the alleged violation occurred in a corporate function or North America. Where the suspected Code violation could amount to criminal conduct, Strategic Security also may take part in the investigation. Human Resources personnel may be informed, but will not take an active role in a Code investigation.

Q   Will the subject of the investigation receive notification of the investigation?

A   It depends on the circumstances and the results of the preliminary investigation. If there is insufficient evidence of a Code violation, the investigation may be closed without notification. In the event it is determined that evidence of a violation exists, the individual will be notified but that notification may not occur until after records have been reviewed and witnesses interviewed.

Q   Will the subject of the investigation have an opportunity to respond to any allegations made against him or her?

A   Yes, the subject of an investigation will have the opportunity to respond to any allegations made against that person.

Q   Can a suspected violator be suspended while an investigation is ongoing?

A   Yes, at the discretion of the Finance or Legal departments, in conjunction with Corporate Audit, a person suspected of violating the Code can be suspended with or without pay while an investigation is conducted.

DECISION

Q   Who makes the decision on whether a violation of the Code has occurred?

A   A preliminary determination will be made by the Finance and Legal departments. That preliminary determination should be communicated to the Principal Manager of the alleged violator and to the Director of Corporate Audit. Sole authority for making a final determination that a violation has occurred rests jointly with the Chief Financial Officer and General Counsel.

DISCIPLINE

Q   Does anyone make a recommendation on appropriate discipline?

A   Yes, the Principal Manager together with the Legal and Finance departments should make a recommendation on appropriate discipline. That recommendation should be given to the Director of Corporate Audit for review and presentation to the Chief Financial Officer and the General Counsel.

Q   What factors will be considered in determining the appropriate punishment?

A   The company uses a system of progressive discipline. The company strives to impose discipline for a code violation that fits the nature and particular facts of a violation, including the history of those involved.

Q   What forms of discipline does the company impose?

A   The company generally will issue warnings or letters of reprimand for less significant, first-time offenses. Violations of a more serious nature may result in suspension without pay, demotion, loss or reduction of bonus or option awards or any combination. Termination of employment generally is reserved for theft or other violations amounting to a breach of trust, and for cases where a person has engaged in multiple violations.

Q   Who makes the final decision on discipline?

A   The final decision on appropriate discipline will be made jointly by the Chief Financial Officer and General Counsel.

Q   Can the violator seek reconsideration of the final discipline decision?

A   Yes, within 14 days of notification of the final discipline decision, the alleged violator can make a written request for reconsideration which will be considered by the General Counsel and Chief Financial Officer.

Q   Who communicates the final discipline decision?

A   The appropriate Principal Manager or representatives from the Legal or Finance departments.

REPORTING AND RECORDKEEPING

Q   Do the Chief Financial Officer and General Counsel report the violation and discipline to anyone other than the violators?

A   Yes. The Chief Financial Officer and General Counsel will report their final decision to the Director of Corporate Audit, who will in turn notify the violator's Principal Manager. The Director of Corporate Audit will also report all final decisions to the Audit Committee of the Board of Directors or its designee.

Q   What documents concerning the violation will be maintained in an employee's personnel records?

A   A notation as to the final decision as well as any letters of reprimand or other communications with the violator will be placed in the employee's personnel file as part of his or her permanent record.

These guidelines do not create any contractual rights
of any kind between The Coca-Cola Company
and its employees. In addition, all employees should
understand that these guidelines do not modify
their employment relationship, whether at will
or governed by contract. The Coca-Cola Company
reserves the rights to amend or alter these guidelines
at any time and for any reason.

ENRON
CODE OF ETHICS
July, 2000

Index

FOREWORD

As officers and employees of Enron Corp., its subsidiaries, and its affiliated companies, we are responsible for conducting the business affairs of the companies in accordance with all applicable laws and in a moral and honest manner.

To be sure that we understand what is expected of us, Enron has adopted certain policies, with the approval of the Board of Directors, which are set forth in this booklet. I ask that you read them carefully and completely and that, as you do, you reflect on your past actions to make certain that you have complied with the policies. It is absolutely essential that you fully comply with these policies in the future. If you have any questions, talk them over with your supervisor, manager, or Enron legal counsel.

We want to be proud of Enron and to know that it enjoys a reputation for fairness and honesty and that it is respected. Gaining such respect is one aim of our advertising and public relations activities, but no matter how effective they may be, Enron's reputation finally depends on its people, on you and me. Let's keep that reputation high.

July 1, 2000

Kenneth L. Lay
Chairman and Chief Executive Officer

HOW TO USE THIS BOOKLET

Enron has long had a set of written policies dealing with rules of conduct to be used in conducting the business affairs of Enron Corp., its subsidiaries, and its affiliated companies (collectively the "Company"). It is very important that you understand the scope of those policies and learn the details of every one that relates to your job.

In order to do this, please take the following steps:

1.   Carefully read the summaries of each of the Enron policies in this booklet;

2.   If you have a concern or question, talk it over with your supervisor, manager, or Enron legal counsel; and/or

3.   Report your concerns or possible violations to the Enron Corp. Compliance Officer as described in the section on Responsibility for Reporting at page 60 of this booklet.

Enclosed with this booklet is a Certificate of Compliance to be signed by you as a statement of your personal agreement to comply with the policies stated herein during the term of your employment with the Company. Please carefully review this booklet, then sign and return the Certificate of Compliance to Elaine V. Overturf, Deputy Corporate Secretary and Director of Stockholder Relations, Enron Corp.

These policies are not an employment contract. The Company does not create any contractual rights by issuing these policies.

The Company reserves the right to amend, alter, and terminate policies at any time.

PRINCIPLES OF HUMAN RIGHTS

As a partner in the communities in which we operate, Enron believes it has a responsibility to conduct itself according to certain basic tenets of human behavior that transcend industries, cultures, economics, and local, regional and national boundaries.

And because we take this responsibility as an international employer and global corporate citizen seriously, we have developed the following principles on human rights.

Enron's Vision and Values are the platform upon which our human rights principles are built.

Vision

Enron's vision is to become the world's leading energy company – creating innovative and efficient energy solutions for growing economies and a better environment worldwide.

Values

Respect

We treat others as we would like to be treated ourselves. We do not tolerate abusive or disrespectful treatment. Ruthlessness, callousness and arrogance don't belong here.

Integrity

We work with customers and prospects openly, honestly and sincerely. When we say we will do something, we will do it; when we say we cannot or will not do something, then we won't do it.

Communication

We have an obligation to communicate. Here, we take the time to talk with one another ... and to listen. We believe that information is meant to move and that information moves people.

Excellence

We are satisfied with nothing less than the very best in everything we do. We will continue to raise the bar for everyone. The great fun here will be for all of us to discover just how good we can really be.

PRINCIPLES OF HUMAN RIGHTS

- Enron stands on the foundation of its Vision and Values. Every employee is educated about the Company's Vision and Values and is expected to conduct business with other employees, partners, contractors, suppliers, vendors and customers keeping in mind respect, integrity, communication and excellence. Everything we do evolves from Enron's Vision and Values statements.

- At Enron, we treat others as we expect to be treated ourselves. We believe in respect for the rights of all individuals and are committed to promoting an environment characterized by dignity and mutual respect for employees, customers, contractors, suppliers, partners, community members and representatives of all levels of Government.

- We do not and will not tolerate human rights abuses of any kind by our employees or contractors.

- We believe in treating all employees fairly, regardless of gender, race, color, language, religion, age, ethic background, political or other opinion, national origin, or physical limitation.

- We are dedicated to conducting business according to all applicable local and international laws and regulations, including, but not limited to, the U.S. Foreign Corrupt Practices Act, and with the highest professional and ethical standards.

- We are committed to operating safely and conducting business worldwide in compliance with all applicable environmental, health, and safety laws and regulations and strive to improve the lives of the people in the regions in which we operate. These laws, regulations, and standards are designed to safeguard the environment, human health, wildlife, and natural resources. Our commitment to observe them faithfully is an integral part of our business and of our values.

- We believe that playing an active role in every community in which we operate fosters a long-term partnership with the people with whom we come into daily contact. Strengthening the communities where our employees live and work is a priority. We focus community relations activities on several areas, with particular emphasis on education, the environment, and promoting healthy families.

- We believe in offering our employees fair compensation through wages and other benefits.

- We believe that our employees and the employees of our contractors working in our facilities should have safe and healthy working conditions.

Education/Communication

Because we take these principles seriously, we should act decisively to ensure that all those with whom we do business understand our policies and standards.

Providing clearly written guidelines reinforces our principles and business ethics. Enron employees at all levels are expected to be active proponents of our principles and to report without retribution anything they observe or discover that indicates our standards are not being met.

Compliance with the law and ethical standards are conditions of employment, and violations will result in disciplinary action, which may include termination. New employees are asked to sign a statement, and employees are periodically asked to reaffirm their commitment to these principles.

Furthermore, Enron's contractors, suppliers, and vendors should be expected to uphold the same respect for human rights that we require of ourselves, and we should seek to include appropriate provisions in every new contract entered with these parties. When we are joint venture partners with other companies, we will work to gain board approval for similar measures in joint venture contracts with contractors, suppliers and vendors.

SECURITIES TRADES BY COMPANY PERSONNEL

No director, officer, or employee of Enron Corp. or its subsidiaries or its affiliated companies (collectively referred to herein as "Company") shall, directly or indirectly, trade in the securities of Enron Corp., Northern Border Partners, L.P., EOTT Energy Partners, L.P., or any other Enron Corp. subsidiary or affiliated company with publicly-traded securities, or any other publicly-held company while in the possession of material non-public information relating to or affecting any such company, disclose such information to others who may trade, or recommend the purchase or sale of securities of a company to which such information relates. Advice should be sought in respect of equivalent requirements under other applicable jurisdictions.

The Need For A Policy Statement

The Securities and Exchange Commission ("SEC") and the Justice Department actively pursue violations of insider trading laws. Historically, their efforts were concentrated on individuals directly involved in trading abuses. In 1988, to further deter insider trading violations, Congress expanded the authority of the SEC and the Justice Department, adopting the Insider Trading and Securities Fraud Enforcement Act (the "Act"). In addition to increasing the penalties for insider trading, the Act puts the onus on companies and possibly other "controlling persons" for violations by company personnel.

Although the Act is aimed primarily at the securities industry, application of the laws may be made to companies in other industries. Many experts have concluded that if companies like Enron Corp. do not take active steps to adopt preventive policies and procedures covering securities trades by Company personnel, the consequences could be severe.

In addition to responding to the Act, we are adopting this Policy Statement to avoid even the appearance of improper conduct on the part of anyone employed by or associated with the

Company (not just so-called insiders). We have all worked hard over the years to establish our reputation for integrity and ethical conduct. We cannot afford to have it damaged.

The Consequences

This policy applies to all employees of the Company. It is intended to provide guidance to employees with respect to existing legal restrictions. It is not intended to result in the imposition of liability on employees that would not exist in the absence of such policy. Any breach of this policy, however, may subject employees to criminal penalties.

The consequences of insider trading violations can be staggering:

For individuals who trade on inside information (or tip information to others):

- A civil penalty of up to three times the profit gained or loss avoided;

- A criminal fine (no matter how small the profit) of up to $1 million; and

- A jail term of up to ten years.

For a company (as well as possibly any supervisory person) that fails to take appropriate steps to prevent illegal trading:

- A civil penalty of the greater of $1 million or three times the profit gained or loss avoided as a result of the employee's violation; and

- A criminal penalty of up to $2.5 million.

Moreover, if an employee violates the Company's insider trading policy, the Company may impose sanctions against such individual, including dismissing him or her for cause.

Our Policy

If a director, officer, or any employee of the Company (as defined herein) has material non-public information relating to Enron Corp., Northern Border Partners, L.P., EOTT Energy Partners, L.P., or any other Enron Corp. subsidiary or affiliated company with publicly-traded securities, it is the Company's policy that neither that person nor any related person may buy or sell securities of Enron Corp., Northern Border Partners, L.P., EOTT Energy Partners, L.P., or other Enron Corp. subsidiary or affiliated company with publicly traded securities, or engage in any other action to take advantage of, or pass on to others, that information. This policy also applies to material non-public information relating to any other company, including our customers or suppliers, obtained in the course of employment.

A transaction that may be necessary or justifiable for independent reasons (such as the need to raise money for an emergency expenditures) does not constitute an exception. Even the appearance of an improper transaction must be avoided to preserve the Company's reputation for adhering to the highest standards of conduct.

Material Information. Material information is any information that a reasonable investor would consider important in a decision to buy, hold, or sell stock: in short, any information which could reasonably be expected to affect the price of the stock. If you are considering buying or selling a security because of information you possess, you should assume such information is material.

Examples. Common examples of information that will frequently be regarded as material are: projections of future earnings or losses; news of a pending or proposed merger, acquisition, or tender offer; news of a significant sale of assets or the disposition of a subsidiary; changes in dividend policies or the declaration of a stock split or the offering of additional securities; changes in management; significant new products or discoveries; impending bankruptcy or financial liquidity problems; and the gain or loss of a substantial customer or supplier. Either positive or negative information may be material. The foregoing list is by no means exclusive.

Twenty-Twenty Hindsight. If your securities transactions become the subject of scrutiny, they will be viewed after-the-fact with the benefit of hindsight. As a result, before engaging in any transaction you should carefully consider how regulators and others might view your transaction in hindsight.

Transactions By Family Members. The very same restrictions apply to your family members and others living in your household. Employees are expected to be responsible for the compliance of their immediate family and personal household.

Tipping Information To Others. Whether the information is proprietary information about the Company or information that could have an impact on our stock prices, employees must not pass material non-public information on to others; this is called tipping. The above penalties may apply, whether or not you derive any direct benefit from another's actions.

When Information Is Public. Information is "non-public" until it has been disseminated in a manner making it available to investors generally. This is typically satisfied by distribution of such information by means of a press release. However, even after such information is released to the press, you should wait a period of time (at least one business day and often two or three business days) before trading or disclosing such information to others. Again, it is a good idea to exercise caution and wait a longer period of time following the release of material information than you might first consider warranted.

Company Assistance

No set of specific rules will be adequate in every circumstance. Any person who has any questions about specific transactions may obtain additional guidance from Elaine Overturf, Deputy Corporate Secretary and Director of Stockholder Relations, at (713) 853-6062, who will consult with Company counsel as appropriate. Remember, however, that the ultimate responsibility for adhering to the Policy Statement and avoiding improper transactions rests with you. In this regard, it is imperative that you act in good faith and use your best judgment.

BUSINESS ETHICS

Employees of Enron Corp., its subsidiaries, and its affiliated companies (collectively the "Company") are charged with conducting their business affairs in accordance with the highest ethical standards. An employee shall not conduct himself or herself in a manner which directly or indirectly would be detrimental to the best interests of the Company or in a manner which would bring to the employee financial gain separately derived as a direct consequence of his or her employment with the Company. Moral as well a legal obligations will be fulfilled openly, promptly, and in a manner which will reflect price on the Company's name.

Products and services of the Company will be of the highest quality and as represented. Advertising and promotion will be truthful, not exaggerated or misleading.

Agreements, whether contractual or verbal, will be honored. No bribes, bonuses, kickbacks, lavish entertainment, or gifts will be given or received in exchange for special position, price, or privilege.

Employees will maintain the confidentiality of the Company's sensitive or proprietary information and will not use such information for their personal benefit.

Employees shall refrain, both during and after their employment, from publishing any oral or written statements about the Company or any of its officers, employees, agents, or representatives that are slanderous, libelous, or defamatory; or that disclose private or confidential information about their business affairs; or that constitute an intrusion into their seclusion or private lives; or that give rise to unreasonable publicity about their private lives; or that place them in a false light before the public; or that constitute a misappropriation of their name or likeness.

Relations with the Company's many publics – customers, stockholders, governments, employees, suppliers, press, and bankers – will be conducted in honesty, candor, and fairness.

It is Enron's policy that each "contract" must be reviewed by one of our attorneys prior to its being submitted to the other parties to such "contract" and that it must be initialed by one of our attorneys prior to being signed. By "contract" we mean each contract, agreement, bid, term sheet, letter of intent, memorandum of understanding, amendment, modification, supplement, fax telex, and other document or arrangement that could reasonably be expected to impose an obligation on any Enron entity. (Certain Enron entities utilize standard forms that have been pre-approved by the legal department to conduct routine activities; so long as no material changes are made to these pre-approved forms, it is not necessary to seek legal review or initialing prior to their being signed.) Please bear in mind that your conduct and/or your conversations may have, under certain circumstances, the unintended effect of creating an enforceable obligation; Consult with the legal department with respect to any questions you may have in this regard.

Additionally, it is Enron's policy that the selection and retention of outside legal counsel be conducted exclusively by the legal department. (Within the legal department, the selection and retention of counsel is coordinated and approved by James V. Derrick Jr., Enron's Executive Vice President and General Counsel.) In the absence of this policy, it would not be possible for our legal department to discharge its obligation to manage properly our relationships with outside counsel.

Employees will comply with the executive stock ownership requirements set forth by the Board of Directors of Enron Corp., if applicable.

Laws and regulations affecting the Company will be obeyed. Even though the laws and business practices of foreign nations may differ from those in effect in the Unites States, the applicability of both foreign and U.S. laws to the Company's operations will be strictly observed. Illegal behavior on the part of any employee in the performance of Company duties will neither be condoned or tolerated.

CONFIDENTIAL INFORMATION AND TRADE SECRETS

Ownership of Information

All information, ideas, concepts, improvements, discoveries, and employee inventions, whether patentable or not, which are conceived, made, developed, or acquired by an employee, individually or in conjunction with others, during the employee's employment by Enron Corp., its subsidiaries, and its affiliated companies (collectively the "Company") (whether during business hours or otherwise and whether on the Company's premises or otherwise) which relate to the Company's business, products or services shall be disclosed to the Company and are and shall be the sole and exclusive property of the Company.

For this purpose, the Company's business, products, or services, include, without limitation, all such information relating to corporate opportunities, research, financial and sales data, pricing and trading terms, evaluations, opinions, interpretations, acquisition prospects, the identity of customers or their requirements, the identity of key contracts within the customer's organization (or within the organization of acquisition prospects), marketing and merchandising techniques, and prospective names and marks.

Moreover, all documents, drawings, memoranda, notes, records, files, correspondence, manuals, models, specifications, computer programs, e-mail, voice mail, electronic databases, maps, and all other writings or materials of any type embodying any of such information, ideas, concepts, improvements, discoveries, and inventions are and shall be the sole and exclusive property of the Company.

If, during an employee's employment by the Company, the employee creates any original work of authorship fixed in any tangible medium of expression which is the subject matter of copyright (such as videotapes, written presentations on acquisitions, computer programs, e-mail, voice mail, electronic databases, drawings, maps, architectural renditions, models, manuals, brochures, or the like) relating to the Company's business, products or services, whether such work is created solely by the employee or jointly with others (whether during business hours or otherwise and whether on Company's premises or otherwise), the employee shall disclose such work to the Company.

The Company shall be deemed to be the author of such work if the work is prepared by the employee in the scope of his or her employment; or, if the work is not prepared by employee within the scope of his or her employment but is specially ordered by the Company as a contribution to a collective work, as a part of a motion picture or other audiovisual work, as a translation, as a supplementary work, as a compilation, or as an instructional text, then the work shall be considered to be work made for hire and the Company shall be deemed to be the author of the work. If such work is neither prepared by the employee within the scope of his or her employment nor a work specially ordered and is deemed to be a work made for hire, then the employee hereby agrees to assign, and by these presents does assign, to the Company all of the employee's worldwide right, title and interest in and to such work and all rights of copyright therein.

Confidential Company Information and Trade Secrets

You may have access to or become aware of confidential and/or proprietary information of the Company - that is, information relating to the Company's business which is not generally or publicly known. This information includes but is not limited to:

> Internal telephone lists and directories, bid, trading, and financial data; planned new projects and ventures; advertising and marketing programs; lists of potential or actual customers and suppliers; wage and salary or other personnel data; capital investment plans; changes in management or policies of the Company's; suppliers prices; and other trade secrets.

The Company's confidential or proprietary information could be very helpful to suppliers and the Company's competitors, to the detriment of the Company. To help protect the Company's interests, business units have established and implemented computer and electronic security measures to ensure that employees have the means to communicate domestically and internationally in a secure fashion. Employees should use these means and, in disclosing or using Company confidential or proprietary information, should follow these guidelines:

- Do not use, either for your own personal benefit or for the benefit of others, Company information that is not publicly known;

- Do not disclose Company proprietary or confidential information to other employees or outsiders, except as required in the conduct of the Company's business;

- Dispose of documents containing the Company's confidential or proprietary information with care so as to avoid inadvertent disclosure; and

- Guard against inadvertently disclosing such information in public discussions where you may be overheard and in discussions with family members.

As a result of the employee's employment by the Company, the employee may also from time to time have access to, or knowledge of, confidential business information or trade secrets of third parties, such as customers, suppliers, partners, joint venturers, and the like of the Company. Each employee agrees to preserve and protect the confidentiality of such third party confidential information and trade secrets to the same extent, and on the same basis, as the Company's confidential business information and trade secrets.

These obligations of confidence apply even if the information has not been reduced to a tangible medium of expression (*e.g.,* is only maintained in the minds of the Company's employees) and, if it has been reduced to a tangible medium, irrespective of the form or medium in which the information is embodied (*e.g.,* documents, drawings, memoranda, notes, records, files, correspondence, manuals, models, specifications, computer programs, e-mail, voice mail, electronic databases, maps, and all other writings or materials of any type).

Information Acquisition

Acquiring and having access to accurate and current market information is of significant interest to the Company. The Company therefore encourages employees to share within the Company potentially useful information they receive. This includes information properly obtained from outside sources. On the other hand, using improper means to obtain trade secret information of others, or using such trade secret information, could expose the Company, or individual employees, to potentially significant civil fines or liabilities, or even criminal penalties. The use of improper means to obtain trade secret information and the use of others' trade secrets is therefore prohibited. This policy explains the types of information that employees are encouraged to obtain and the types of activities they can pursue in obtaining information, as well as the types of improper activities to obtain trade secret information that they are prohibited from engaging in.

Publicly Available Information. A vast amount of information is freely available to the public and the acquisition and use of this type of information is encouraged. Publicly available information includes information:

- found in books and magazines;

- available on the internet;

- made public by federal, state, or local government agencies;

- revealed in legal filings and pleadings;

- disclosed or discussed in public places, at conferences or trade shows, or in specialized trade or technical publications;

- contained in patent applications or issued patents; and

- obtainable from simple observation from the street or another legally permissible location.

While all of this information is publicly available, it is not necessarily widely known. To the degree that this information could have particular relevance to the Company, employees are encouraged to find this information and share it within the Company.

"Trade Secret" Information. Generally, information is considered a "trade secret" only if:

- the information is in fact secret, *i.e.*, not generally known to and not readily ascertainable by the public;

- the owner has taken reasonable measures to keep the information secret; and

- the information has independent economic value because it is not widely known.

In 1996, the U.S. Congress passed the Economic Espionage Act which makes it a crime to steal trade secrets. More specifically, the Economic Espionage Act prohibits you from acquiring trade secrets of others through improper means, such as deceit or misrepresentations, and prohibits the receipt or use of information illegally acquired by a third party, or from present or former employees who are not authorized to disclose it. The Economic Espionage Act provides for criminal fines for the Company of up to $10 million and criminal fines for an employee of up to $500,000 and up to 15 years imprisonment. Accordingly, an employee should not knowingly:

(1) take, carry away, or obtain a third party trade secret without authorization or obtain a third party trade secret by fraud or deception;

(2) copy, download, mail, deliver, send, transmit, or communicate a third party trade secret without authorization; or

(3) receive, buy, or possess a third party trade secret knowing it has been stolen or obtained without authorization.

Non-Public, Non- "Trade Secret" Information. Certain information is not "public" in the sense that it is not published or widely available to the public, but neither is it a "trade secret". This would include, for example, information about a company that the Company itself made no effort to keep secret. Nothing would bar an employee from obtaining such information in a casual conversation and subsequently reporting or using that information. Accordingly, Company employees are encouraged to obtain, share, and use such non-public secret information, *provided* that no improper means are used. If improper means are necessary to obtain information, a good chance exists that the party who would divulge the information knows that he or she should keep the information secret, thus raising the likelihood that the information could be considered a trade secret. "Improper Means" would include:

- lying, engaging in deception, or creating a false impression in order to induce the disclosure of trade secrets;

- paying someone to reveal trade secrets;

- blackmailing or threatening someone to reveal trade secrets;

- paying someone who had already improperly obtained trade secrets to reveal those secrets to you; and

- engaging in any activity that is itself illegal (such as theft or computer "hacking") in order to obtain secrets.

The preceding list is not exhaustive. Other types of activity engaged in to obtain trade secrets could be considered "improper." Therefore, if you have any doubts about activities you are thinking of pursuing to obtain information, *do not engage in those activities* until you have first discussed them with the Company's General Counsel. Only if you have first obtained the advice and clearance of the Company's General Counsel may you engage in any activity of a questionable nature to obtain information from others.

Copyright and Trademark

The federal Copyright Act provides for criminal fines for an employee up of to $250,000 and up to 5 years imprisonment for the first offense. The federal Trademark Counterfeiting Act provides for criminal fines for the Company or up to $1 million and criminal fines for an employee of up to $250,000 and up to 5 years imprisonment for the first offense.

An employee will not willfully infringe for purposes of commercial advantage or private financial gain a third party's copyright in a work by copying the work, distributing copies of the work, using the work to prepare derivative works, or in the case of some works, by publicly displaying or performing the work. Similarly, an employee will not intentionally traffic in goods or services using a counterfeit or spurious trademark.

Conclusion and Summary

Each employee agrees to act with honesty, candor and fairness with respect to competitors and third parties and to comply in all respects with applicable laws prohibiting the misappropriation of trade secrets, copyright infringement, or use of counterfeit or spurious trademarks. Under no circumstance will any activity be authorized or undertaken by an employee which violates the federal Economic Espionage Act, the federal Copyright Act, the federal Trademark Counterfeiting Act, or any other applicable domestic or foreign laws.

If an employee has any questions concerning the meaning of the laws summarized in this Policy, the employee should contact the Company's General Counsel.

Upon signing the Certificate of Compliance, an employee acknowledges and agrees that:

1. the business of the Company is highly competitive, and its strategies, methods, books, records, and documents, its technical information concerning its products, equipment, services, and processes, procurement, procedures and pricing techniques, and the names of and other information

(such as credit and financial data) concerning its customers and its business affiliates all comprise confidential business information and trade secrets which are valuable, special, and unique assets which the Company uses in its business to obtain a competitive advantage over its competitors;

2. the protection of such confidential business information and trade secrets against unauthorized disclosure and use is of critical importance to the Company in maintaining its competitive position;

3. he or she will not, at any time during or after his or her employment by the Company, make any unauthorized disclosure of any confidential business information or trade secrets of the Company, or make any use thereof, except in the carrying out of his or her employment responsibilities hereunder;

4. the Company shall be a third party beneficiary of the employee's obligations under this policy; and

5. he or she agrees to act with honesty, candor, and fairness with respect to competitors and third parties and to comply in all respects with applicable laws prohibiting the misappropriation of trade secrets, copyright infringement, or the use of counterfeit or spurious trademarks.

All documents, drawings, memoranda, notes, records, files, correspondence, manuals, models, specifications, computer programs, e-mail, voice mail, electronic databases, maps, and all other writings or materials of any type made by, or coming into possession of, employee during the period of employee's employment by the Company which contain or disclose confidential business information or trade secrets of the Company shall be and remain the property of the Company. Upon termination of employee's employment by the Company, for any reason, employee promptly shall deliver the same, and all copies thereof, to the Company.

SAFETY

Employees of the Company have a responsibility to comply with all applicable laws and regulations regarding the safe design, construction, maintenance, and operation of Company facilities. It is the responsibility of every employee to perform his or her work and to conduct the Company's operations in a safe manner. Employees should be aware that health and safety laws may provide for significant civil and criminal penalties against individuals and/or the Company for failure to comply with applicable requirements. Accordingly, each employee must comply with all applicable safety and health laws, rules, and regulations, including occupational safety and health standards.

POLICY ON USE OF COMMUNICATION SERVICES AND EQUIPMENT

The term "Communication Services and Equipment" as used in this Policy and the accompanying Procedures shall mean any and all communications systems or equipment owned or possessed by Enron Corp., its divisions, its subsidiaries, and its affiliated and related companies (the "Company"), or used in connection with the Company's business, including but not limited to, telephones, facsimile machines, computers, computer modems, special long-distance services, cellular phones, voice mail, pagers, electronic mails, mail and delivery services, storage means of all types for the physical or electronic storage of the Company's information or data, transaction services, or any other services of any nature whatsoever in connection with any communication systems necessary or desirable to promote the conduct of the Company's business.

General application of this Policy and the accompanying Procedures

This Policy and the accompanying Procedures apply to all employees, third party contractors, guests, licensees, or invitees of the Company who utilize, possess, or have access to the Company's Communication Services and Equipment (cumulatively referred to herein as the "Users" of the Company's Communication Services and Equipment).

General Policy of the Company with respect to its Communication Services and Equipment

It is the general policy of Company:

- To provide or contract for effective Communication Services and Equipment for use by the Company in connection with its business;

- To preserve and protect the confidentiality of the information and data of the Company and its customers and contractors;

- To preserve and protect the legal privileges provided by the law with respect to attorney/client communications, work product, and investigations of the Company and its customers and contractors; and

- To operate and maintain the Company's Communication Services and Equipment in a manner that is in full compliance with the law.

Limits on expectations of privacy

All Users of the Company's Communication Services and Equipment are advised and placed on notice that:

1. The United States government, and the various State and local governments, may monitor contemporaneous communications of all types (including communication by telephone, facsimile machine, computer modems, special long-distance services, cellular phones, voice mail, pages, electronic mail, mail, and other delivery services) or access stored communications, data, or information of all types, subject to the protections of the Fourth Amendment of the Unites States Constitution, which generally requires the issuance of a court order or warrant. Moreover, the United States government, and the various State and local governments, may monitor contemporaneous oral, wire, or electronic communications of all types subject to federal statues such as the First Amendment Privacy Protection Act and the Omnibus Crime Control and Safe Streets Act, as amended by the Electronic Communications Private Act of 1986.

2. The Federal Rules of Civil Procedure and the rules of civil procedure for almost all States permit requests for production of documents that are likely to lead to the discovery of relevant evidence. Both the Federal Rules of Civil Procedure and the Texas Rules of Civil Procedure specifically allow the discovery of electronically maintained data. For example, Rule 34 of the Federal Rules of Civil Procedure and

Rule 166b(2)(b) of the Texas Rules of Civil Procedure permit the discovery of data compilations from which information can be obtained and, if necessary, translated by the respondent through detective devices into reasonably readable form.

3. There should be no expectations of privacy with respect to communications sent to or received from public electronic bulletin boards or public electronic communications systems such as the Internet.

4. Under the regulations of the United States Postal Service, any mail addressed to a non-governmental organization, including but not limited to corporations, firms, sole proprietorships, partnerships, joint ventures, and associations, or to an individual, such as an official, employee, contractor, client, agent, etc. by name or title at the address of the organization, shall be delivered to the organization. This is also true with respect to mail addressed in this manner to former officials, employees, contractors, agents, clients, etc. Moreover, mail addressed in this manner but bearing the term "personal" is no different from other mail and will be delivered by the United States Postal Service to the Company. For example, the United States Postal Service will deliver each of the following to the offices of the Company:

Sam Smith Enron Corp. 1400 Smith Street P.O. Box 1188 Houston, Texas 77251	Sam Smith 1400 Smith Street Houston, Texas 77251	Sam Smith Personal and Confidential P.O. Box 1188 Houston, Texas 77251

All such mail belongs to the Company until such time as the Company determines that the information contained in the mail does not pertain to the business of the Company. The Company has the right to open the mail if there is some question as to its deliverability and/or to forward the mail to a superior or Company designated recipient if the person to whom the mail is addressed is no longer with the Company or is ill or on extended leave. Moreover, all incoming or outgoing mail containing information owned by the Company is the property of the Company, and the Company has the right to open any Company mail to protect its business interests or to prevent illegal conduct.

5. The Company reserves the right to monitor on a continuous basis the contemporaneous communications of certain of its functions, such as communications conducted on the telephone used in connection with certain training functions and communications conducted on the telephone on the floors in which certain of its traders operate. There should be no expectation of privacy by anyone with respect to communications conducted on those telephones.

6. The Company reserves the right to monitor on a contemporaneous basis communications transmitted by or stored within its Communication Services and Equipment in the ordinary course of the Company's business to ensure that no improper, illegal, or criminal activities are being conducted. Such monitoring shall be effected in accordance with the provisions of the Omnibus Crime Control and Safe Streets Act, as amended by the Electronic Communications Privacy Act of 1986 and shall be effected only if authorized by an officer of the Company.

7. The Company reserves the right to delete or destroy any and all communications, including E-mail and voice mail messages, stored in the Company's Communication

Services and Equipment. As a general rule, the Company's Communication Services and Equipment is not backed-up and should therefore, be thought of as a very temporary storage media. If a machine failure in the Company's Communication Services and Equipment occurs, all messages and data could be lost. Therefore, Users must not consider E-mail and voice mail messages to be permanently stored by the Company. On the other hand, the Company also reserves the right in its discretion to maintain any and all communications, including E-mail and voice mail messages, transmitted by or stored within the Company's Communication Services and Equipment. Users therefore also should take care that the messages they transmit or store comply with all of the Company's policies and with the law.

8. The Company reserves the right to access E-mail messages, voice mail messages, data, or information stored on the Company's computers or other electronic devices or media owned or controlled by the Company or comprising the Company's Communication Services and Equipment. Therefore, there should be no expectation of privacy with respect to such stored E-mail messages, voice mail messages, data, or information.

9. Because all of the Company's Communication Services and Equipment are the property of the Company, the Company reserves the right to monitor its Communication Services and Equipment to ensure that its property is being properly and legally used.

10. Users do not have a personal privacy right in any data or information created, received, or sent on the Company's Communication Services and Equipment. Any data or information transmitted or stored on the Company's Communication Services and Equipment, whether or not they relate or pertain to the Company's business, goods, or services, may be accessed by the Company. Any employee or contractor who elects to utilize the Company's Communication Services and Equipment to transmit or store data or information recognizes that the Company may access and monitor such data or information and has no obligation to continue to store such data and information.

Ownership and confidentiality of information

1. All of the Company's Communication Services and Equipment are the property of the Company. Any and all communication, data, or information created, received, or sent on the Company's Communication Services and Equipment are the property of the Company. Users have no right, title, or interest in such Communication Services and Equipment or in any communications, data, or information created, received, or sent on the Company's Communication Services and Equipment. All means of identifying communications, such as the use of domain names on the Internet or other networks or systems, that embody or use the Company's image, names, or marks (such as an Internet domain name incorporating Enron.Com) shall belong to the Company.

2. This Policy and the accompanying Procedures do not modify in any way the Company's policy that the Company is and remains the owner of all information created by the Company's employees during their employment by the Company that relates to business, goods, or services of the Company, irrespective of where such

information is stored or maintained, *e.g.,* in electronic form on the hard drives of the Company's computers, in electronic form in servers maintained by the Company as part of its network, or in diskettes or computers purchased by the Company that are possessed by the employees.

3. This Policy and the accompanying Procedures do not modify in any way the Company's policy that Users remain obligated to protect the confidentiality of the Company's information irrespective of where such information is stored or maintained, *e.g.,* in electronic form on the hard drives of the Company's computers, in electronic form on the hard drives of the Company's computers, in electronic form in servers maintained by the Company as part of its network, or in diskettes or computers purchased by the Company that are possessed by the employees.

The right to use the Company's Communication Services and Equipment is at the will of the Company and is conditioned on continued compliance with the Company's rules and policies

1. Users are allowed to utilize the Company's Communication Services and Equipment only at the will and discretion of the Company. The Company has the right to prohibit Users from utilizing the Company's Communication Services and Equipment at any time for any reason.

2. Moreover, the Users' right to use the Company's Communication Services and Equipment is conditioned on acceptance of the terms of the Policy and the accompanying Procedures as well as continued compliance with this and all of the Company's other rules and policies.

Acceptance, disciplinary action, interpretation and modification

Employment by the Company, agreement by a contractor to do business with the Company, or use of the Company" Communication Services and Equipment by a User each constitutes acceptance of and consent to the terms of this Policy and the accompanying Procedures.

Improper use of the Company's Communication Services and Equipment may result in discipline, up to and including termination.

Questions about interpretation of this Policy and the accompanying Procedures should be referred to the Company's Legal Department.

Purpose

To set forth the procedures for the use of the Company's Communication Services and Equipment in accordance with the Policy.

General application of the Policy and these Procedures

The *Policy* and these *Procedures* apply to all Users of the Company's Communication Services and Equipment.

Requirements for the use of the Company's Communication Services and Equipment

1. The Company's Communication Services and Equipment should be used for Company purposes only. Employees should limit use of the Company's Communication Services and Equipment for personal purposes to those

135

circumstances where such personal use enhances such employee's efficiency during office hours or otherwise does not detract from such employee's activities on behalf of the Company. When personal usage is unavoidable, employees must properly log any user chargers and reimburse the Company for them. However, whenever possible, personal communications that incur user charges should be placed on a collect basis or charged directly to the employee's personal credit card or account. Users may not use the Company's Communication Services and Equipment for non-Company businesses, such as "moonlighting" jobs.

2. Users should not utilize the Company's Communication Services and Equipment to send or receive private, personal message they do not wish monitored or accessed by the government, third parties, or the Company.

3. Users shall refrain absolutely from any activity that may cause harm or damage to the Company's Communication Services and Equipment or any communications, data, or information transmitted by or stored within such Communication Services and Equipment.

4. Users may not use the Company's Communication Services and Equipment for or in connection with any illegal or criminal activity. Users may not use the Company's Communication Services and Equipment for any activity which violates any Company policy. For example, Users may not use the Company's Communication Services and Equipment to copy, duplicate, or use software that is not properly licensed or the use of which infringes the copyright of a third party. Users may not use the Company's Communication Services and Equipment to infringe third party intellectual property rights. Accordingly, Users should download information and software from the Internet and other public or third party systems into communications systems and equipment only when such downloads do not infringe on third party copyrights or intellectual property rights.

5. No confidential or proprietary information of the Company and no privileged communications (*e.g.,* attorney/client communications) may be transmitted via public electronic communication systems unless the transmissions are properly encrypted and no third party copyright or intellectual property rights are violated.

6. Users may not use the Company's Communication Services and Equipment to forward messages without a legitimate business purpose under circumstances likely to lead to embarrassment of the sender or to violate a clearly expressed desire of the sender to restrict additional dissemination.

7. Users may not connect incompatible equipment to the Company's Communication Services and Equipment. Users may not use in the Company's Communication Services and Equipment any software that is infected with a virus. If any such software is found to be infected with a virus, Users will immediately alert those who have received a copy and will work with their systems management to remove the virus.

8. Employees and contractors must understand that whatever they reduce to a tangible form and maintain in their physical or electronic files may possibly, under the appropriate circumstances, be discovered by third parties in litigation. Employees and contractors are cautioned that all such documents must comply with the Company's policies with respect to the protection of confidential information, the

Company's policies with respect to the protection of privileged communications, and the Company's document retention policies.

9.   Users may not use the Company's Communication Services and Equipment to transmit "chain" letters.

10.   Users should keep the number of messages and data stored in the Company's Communication Services and Equipment under control and should purge old Communication Services and Equipment messages and data regularly.

11.   Employees should exercise care so that no personal correspondence appears to be an official communication of the Company. Personalized Company stationery and business cards may only be issued by the Company and may only be used in connection with Company business. Employees may not use the Company's address for receiving personal mail or use Company stationery or postage for personal matters.

Passwords

Users must change their passwords every 60 days. Passwords must be no shorter than six characters and must be a mixture of alpha, special, and numeric symbols so that the password code is difficult for others to determine using "password cracking" software.

Passwords should not contain any codes, names, words, or phrases that someone familiar with the owner might associate with that person and thereby have an advantage in cracking the code and using it illegally.

Passwords are not to be shared by two or more people Each User should have a unique code that only he or she knows.

Files containing User account names, log on codes, and passwords (*i.e.,* security files) in Company Communication Services and Equipment should be examined at least weekly for persons who no longer work for the Company, and their access authority should be removed immediately.

Users who have not used their access identification code and password for longer than 90 consecutive calendar days should have their need for continued access reviewed at least monthly.

All Company Communication Services and Equipment that allow persons to connect to the service or equipment from a remote location (dial-up access) should require all Users to authenticate themselves through the sue of passwords or other types of technology, such as voice recognition systems, that ensure the person is who he or she claims to be.

Whenever possible, all remote access Company Communication Services and Equipment should have a preset maximum number of attempts to authenticate the remote User, *e.g.,* 3 attempts. Failure to successfully remotely authenticate within the preset maximum number of attempts should result in the access session being terminated or forwarded to a Company security officer for verification of the requesting party.

Monitoring communication services and equipment access

All Company Communication Services and Equipment should be designed/equipped to accurately and quickly determine and log all attempted or successful intrusions of the system or network by someone not authorized to sue that system or network. Any such "hacker" attempts should be immediately investigated and measures should be taken quickly to prevent that type of unauthorized access in the future.

INTERNET SECURITY POLICY:
SCOPE OF USE OF ELECTRONIC MEDIA AND SERVICES

Introduction – General Application of this Policy

This Internet Security Policy defines roles, responsibilities, and policies for the Company's employees, agents, and contractors using the Company's communications facilities to access third party electronic media and services such as the Internet.

As an advanced technology company, we increasingly use and exploit electronic forms of communication and information exchange. Company employees, agents, and contractors may have access to one or more forms of electronic media and services, computers, e-mail, telephones, voicemail, fax machines, external electronic bulletin boards, wire services, on-line services, and the Internet. The Company encourages the use of these media and associated services because information technology is part of our business, because they make communication more efficient and effective, and because they are valuable sources of information about vendors, customers, new products, and services. However, Company-provided access to electronic media and services (*e.g.,* an Internet account) are the Company's property, and their purpose is to facilitate Company business.

Because of the rapidly changing nature of electronic media, and because the "netiquette" is developing among users of external on-line services and the Internet, this Internet Policy cannot lay down rules to cover every situation. Instead, this Internet Policy expresses the Company's philosophy and sets forth general principles to be applied to the use of electronic media and services. This Internet Policy applies to all Company employees, agents, and contractors using electronic media and services which are: accessed on or from Company premises; accessed using Company computer equipment or via Company-paid access methods; and/or used in a manner which identifies the individual with the Company. Collectively, and individually, such individuals will be referred to in this Policy as "Internet Users".

Use of Company-provided access to the Internet is intended to be primarily for the Company's business-related purposes. Internet access is monitored, and actual web-site connections are recorded. Excessive use of Company-provided access to the Internet for non-business-related purposes will result in loss of access privileges.

Procedures, Guidelines, and Restrictions

Accounts and Accounts Passwords

(a)   Internet Users are responsible for the security of their account password(s) and will be held responsible for all use or misuse of their account. Internet Users must maintain secure passwords to their account. Internet Users accessing the Internet over a Company network may be required to use an ID and password at the firewall (in addition to their usual LAN sign on). Passwords are machine generated and will be changed every thirty days. Internet Users must follow all directions of the Company's system administrators with respect to security of passwords and take reasonable precautions against unauthorized access.

(b)   Remote login to the Company network is prohibited unless permission to do so is granted. Do not remotely log into (or otherwise use) any workstation or computer not designated explicitly for public logins over the Company network - even if the configuration of the computer permits remote access - unless you have explicit permission from the owner and the current user of that computer to log into that machine.

(c)   Access to selected Internet hosts or networks which the Company designates as inappropriate may be denied. You may not use any account set up for another Internet User and you may not attempt to find out the password of a service for which you have not been authorized, including accounts set up for other Internet Users.

       (i)   File Transfer Protocol ("FTP") may be used to initiate transfer of data from/to specified Company hosts and from/to selected Internet hosts. Initiation of FTP sessions to Company hosts from the Internet is prohibited.

       (ii)   Access to "network news" is allowed with restrictions. The Company will apply filters as appropriate to block certain news groups.

       (iii)   Access to the "World Wide Web" is permitted. Inappropriate sites may be blocked from the Company network.

       (iv)   All services not explicitly allowed are prohibited. Use of games or other non-work related objects over the Internet is prohibited.

(d)   Network services and World Wide Web sites can and do monitor access and usage and can identify at least which company - and often which specific individual - is accessing their services. Thus, accessing a particular bulletin board or Website leaves Company-identifiable electronic "tracks" even if the Internet User merely reviews or downloads the material and does not post any message. As a general rule, all Internet use should be conducted with this in mind so as to always portray the Company as a reputable company and to maintain its reputation and goodwill.

Intended Uses

Electronic media and services are primarily for Company business use. All Company systems and related equipment are intended for the communication, transmission, processing, and storage of Company-authorized information. Limited, occasional, or incidental use of electronic media (sending or receiving) for personal, non-business purposes is understandable and acceptable - as is the case with personal phone calls. However, Internet Users need to demonstrate a sense of responsibility and may not abuse the privilege.

Assuring Ethical and Legal Uses

(a)   Electronic media may not be used for knowingly transmitting, retrieving, or storing any communication which is (i) discriminatory, harassing, or threatening, (ii) derogatory to any individual, (iii) obscene, (iv) defamatory, (v) a "chain letter" or junk mail, (vi) untrue or fraudulent, (vii) illegal or against Company policy or contrary to the Company's interest, or (viii) for personal profit.

(b)   In downloading any material from the World Wide Web or by FTP transfer, or in distributing any material by e-mail or FTP transfer, you must bear in mind any proprietary or intellectual property rights of third parties in the material. You must not and may not copy material where such copying would infringe the proprietary or intellectual property rights of third parties. Such infringement is an offense which may render you liable for civil claims and, where appropriate, may also be a criminal offense.

(c)   You may not download or store any indecent or obscene material from the World Wide Web, or any such material received by e-mail or by FTP transfer, and you may not distribute any such material by FTP transfer or by e-mail.

(d)   No e-mail or other electronic communications may be sent which attempt to hide the identity of the sender or represent the sender as someone else or as someone from another company. Whenever Internet Users send e-mail, Internet User name, Internet User ID, and the Company's name are included in each e-mail message. Internet Users are solely responsible for all electronic mail originating from their Internet User id. When using the Company's e-mail facilities, the following are prohibited: (i) forgery or attempted forgery of e-mail messages; and (ii) reading, deleting, copying, or modifying the e–mail of others.

(e)   Employees must respect the confidentiality of other people's electronic communications and may not attempt to (i) "hack" into third party systems, (ii) read other people's logins or "crack" passwords, (iii) breach computer or network security measures, or (iv) intercept or monitor electronic files or communications of other employees or third parties, except by explicit direction of Company management.

(f)   Many software programs and computer data, and related materials such as documentation, are owned by individual users or other companies and are protected by copyright and other laws, together with licenses and other contractual arrangements. Anyone obtaining electronic access t another company's or individual's materials must respect all rights (including copyrights) therein, and may not copy, retrieve, modify, disclose, examine, rename, or forward such materials except as permitted by the person owning the data, software programs, and/or other materials. Such restrictions include:

    (i)   copying programs or data;

    (ii)   reselling programs or data;

    (iii)   using programs or data for non-Company business purposes;

    (iv)   using programs or data for personal financial gain;

    (v)   using programs or data without being one of the licensed individuals or groups; and

    (vi)   publicly disclosing information about software programs without the owner's permission.

FAILURE TO ABIDE BY THESE RESTRICTIONS MAY SUBJECT EMPLOYEES TO CIVIL AND/OR CRIMINAL PROSECUTION.

Consent to Monitoring

Electronic information created and/or communicated by an Internet User using e-mail, word processing, utility programs, spreadsheets, voicemail, telephones, Internet/Bulletin Board System (BBS) access, etc. may be monitored by the Company, and the Company reserves the right to engage in monitoring activities:

(a)   The Company routinely monitors usage patterns for both voice and data communications (*e.g.,* number called or site accessed; call length; times of day when calls were initiated). Reasons include cost analysis/allocation and the management of our gateway to the Internet.

(b)   The Company also reserves the right, in its discretion, and the employee upon signing the Certificate of Compliance consents to such action from the Company, to review and disclose any electronic files and messages (including e-mail) and usage to the extent necessary to ensure that electronic media and services are being used in compliance with the law and with this and other Company policies. The company may also find it necessary to monitor the system for signs of illegal or unauthorized entry. Accordingly, the Company reserves the right, in its discretion, and the undersigned hereby consents to such action by the Company, to intercept and disclose any electronic files and messages (including e-mail) at any time with or without prior notification to the users or owners of such files or resources. The undersigned hereby waives any right to privacy in such electronic files.

(c)   Employees should therefore understand that electronic communications are not totally private and confidential. Sensitive or confidential information should be transmitted by more secure means.

Assuring Proper Use of The Company's System Resources

Electronic media and services should be used in an efficient and economical manner and not in a way that is likely to cause network congestion or significantly hamper the ability of other people to access and use the Company's computer systems. Any software that is designed to destroy data, provide unauthorized access to the Company's computer systems, or disrupt computing processes is prohibited.

Confidentiality and Encryption

In accordance with the Policy on Use of Communication Services and Equipment, Internet Users will maintain the confidentiality of the Company's confidential and/or proprietary information and will not use such information for their personal benefit. Any messages or information sent by an Internet User to one of more individuals via an electronic network (*e.g.,* bulletin board, on-line service, or Internet) are statements identifiable and attributable to the Company. While some users include personal "disclaimers" in electronic messages, it should be noted that there would still be a connection with the Company, and the statement might still be legally imputed to the Company. All communications sent by employees via a network must comply with this and other Company policies and may not disclose any confidential and/or proprietary Company information.

Protecting information that is material to Enron's business decision making is a vital part of maintaining our competitive edge. To that end, Enron will take steps to protect proprietary information while insuring that the necessary transparency for an information-driven business in maintained.

In keeping with the Policy on Use of Communication Services and Equipment, Enron employees, contractors, and consultants are prohibited from posting or otherwise contributing Enron related information to internet message/bulletin boards. Additionally, access to certain internet sites through Enron IT Systems may be monitored or restricted.

To ensure the Company's continuous access to information on the Company's computer systems, no Internet User shall use personal hardware or software to encrypt any e-mail, voicemail, or any other data stored in or communicated by the company's computer systems, except in accordance with express prior written permission from the Company's management. Should an Internet User have a need to use security measurers to encrypt any e-mail, voicemail, or any other data stored in or communicated by the Company's computer systems, such Internet User should contact the appropriate information systems personnel to assist in and facilitate such encryption. The Company will retain the encryption keys for all encrypted data stored in or communicated by the Company's computer systems, except in accordance with express prior written permission from the Company's management. Because there may be a need for the Company to access an Internet User's system or files when he/she is away from the office, Company management, at their discretion, may request that authorized systems personnel reset the password of an Internet User who uses any security measures on an Company-supplied PC, Macintosh, UNIX workstation, or any other Company-supplied workstation for Company use if required.

To meet the Company's public disclosure responsibilities as required by the Securities and Exchange Commission and to ensure that we are communicating a consistent message, public disclosure restrictions apply to interactions over the Internet as well as any other methods of communications. Any employee found to be abusing the privilege of Company-facilitated access to electronic media or services will be subject to corrective action up to an including termination and will risk losing Internet User privileges for himself/herself and possibly for other employees.

Any unauthorized attempts to penetrate or subvert Company computer systems will be thoroughly and promptly investigated and resolved on a case-by-case basis. If circumstances warrant, such attempts will be vigorously pursued and prosecuted to the full extent of the law.

GOVERNMENTAL AFFAIRS AND POLITICAL CONTRIBUTIONS

The Company's official policy concerning all governmental, political, and public matters in which the Company has an interest shall be determined and announced by the Executive Committee of Enron Corp.'s Board of Directors. No alteration of or deviation from such official policy will be made without the approval of the Chairman of the Board and Chief Executive Officer of Enron Corp.

The Company employs governmental relations and public policy personnel who are assigned the responsibility of fulfilling its corporate public affairs responsibility, communicating with public bodies and officials pertaining to the Company's position on public policy questions, and maintaining the goodwill and understanding of public officials.

Communications of the Company's position to public officials or bodies by personnel of the Company and its subsidiaries must be coordinated with the governmental relations and public policy personnel at corporate headquarters.

The Company may also provide factual information to employees and stockholders concerning the impact on the Company of specific issues, legislation, and other governmental, political, and public matters. Such communications must be approved by the Chairman of the Board and Chief Executive Officer of Enron Corp. or the President and Chief Operating Officer of Enron Corp.

To establish restrictions with regard to corporate participation in the political system as imposed by law, the following guidelines will be followed:

1. No funds, assets, or services of the Company will be used for political contributions, directly or indirectly, unless allowed by applicable foreign and U.S. law and approved in advance by the Chairman of the Board or President of Enron.

2. If eligible under applicable foreign and U.S. Law, Company contributions to support or oppose public referenda or similar ballot issues are permitted, but only with advance approval of the Chairman of the Board or President of Enron Corp.

3. Employees, if eligible under applicable foreign and U.S. law, may make political contributions through legally established Company sponsored and approved political support funds. Any such personal contribution is not a deductible expense for federal or other applicable income tax purposes and is not eligible for reimbursement by the Company as a business expense. Political action committees are permitted under U.S. law

Under no circumstances will any activity by authorized or undertaking by an employee which violates the provisions of the Foreign Corrupt Practices Act, federal an state election laws, bribery, or other applicable domestic or foreign laws.

The Company encourages its employees, management and stockholders to exercise their voting rights and take and active interest and participate in public affairs at local, state and national levels.

Employees, regardless of their Company position, are free to express their views on public affairs matters through political or non-political measures of their choice and engage in partisan political activities. Employees should conduct themselves in contacts with others so as to make clear that the views express are their own and not those of the Company.

CONSULTING FEES, COMMISSIONS, AND OTHER PAYMENTS

Agreements with consultants, agents, or representatives must be in writing and must state the services to be performed, the fee basis, amounts to be paid, and other material terms and conditions, and the form and content must be approved by the Company's legal counsel and with respect to foreign consultants, agents, or representatives by Mr. Jack Urquhart, Senior Advisor to the Chairman of the Board of Enron Corp. Payments must bear a reasonable relationship to the value of the services rendered, must be completely documented and recorded, and must not violate the provisions of the Foreign Corrupt Practices Act or any other applicable law, including, without limitation, those relating to bribery. Payments will be made by check or wire transfer in accordance with the following procedure:

143

1.   In any lawful currency in the country where the services are performed; and

2.   To the person directly or to the person's bank account in the country where the services are performed; provided, however, that payment may be made other than in the place of performance with the approval of the Company legal counsel.

When payments are requested to be made in any manner, currency, or place other than in accordance with the above procedure, the person who has made such request shall be advised that such payments shall not be made except upon notification to the governments of both the country of residence and the country where the services are performed, unless Company legal counsel determines that such notice is not required by law and is not otherwise advisable under the circumstances. Such notification shall be made to both governments even though the requested manner of payment does not apparently violate applicable domestic or foreign law. Notification with respect to the requested manner of payment should normally be made to the tax, finance, or other governmental authorities, as shall be appropriate under the circumstances.

The Company policy discourages but does not prohibit customary expediting payments to low-level employees of foreign governments, properly recorded in the Company's books, which are not excessive in amount and which meet the following criteria:

1.   The making of such payments is an established and well-organized practice in the area.

2.   Such payments are to expedite or assure performance of a routine governmental action (such as obtaining customs clearances, visas, and work permits) to which the Company or the Company's employee is clearly entitled.

3.   The payment does not violate any provisions of the Foreign Corrupt Practices Act or any applicable law, including, without limitation, those relating to bribery.

COMPLIANCE WITH THE FOREIGN CORRUPT PRACTICES ACT

The United States Foreign Corrupt Practices Act (the "Act") applies to the Company in its worldwide operations as well as individually to all Company employees with respect to their worldwide activities. The Act prohibits the corrupt offer, payment or gift of money or anything of value to a foreign governmental official or employee or to any foreign political candidate or party for the purpose of influencing any act or decision of a governmental body in order to obtain or retain business, to direct business to any person, or to secure any improper advantage. The Act also prohibits the offer, payment, or gift of money or anything of value to any third party with knowledge that all or a portion of such money or thing of value will be transferred to a governmental official or employee or political candidate for a prohibited purpose. The Act contains certain narrow affirmative defenses to its prohibitions.

The Act provides for stiff criminal and civil penalties. Criminal fees of up to $2,500,000 or twice the gain per offense can be imposed on the Company. Individuals may be imprisoned for up to 10 years per violation and may have to pay criminal fines ranging from $1,000,000 to twice the gain from the violation. In addition, a civil penalty of $10,000 per violation may be imposed on both the Company and any individual. The Company will not reimburse any fine paid by any individual. Accordingly, Company policy requires strict compliance with the Act.

Due to the broad nature of the Act's prohibitions, it may be implicated by a wide range of activities in addition to direct bribery of a foreign official. For instance, arrangements with foreign joint venture partners, foreign agency or sponsorship arrangements, and any direct dealings with, including lavish entertainment of, foreign governmental officials or employees may raise issues under the Act.

Any questions with respect to the application of the Act to any proposed activity by the Company should be referred immediately to Company legal counsel.

COMPLIANCE WITH ANTITRUST LAWS

All employees of the Company are expected to comply fully with all applicable federal, state, and foreign antitrust laws. Whenever any exists as to the legality of any action or arrangement, such transaction must be submitted to Company legal counsel for prior approval and continuing review. Both the spirit and the letter of antitrust laws are to be followed, so as to avoid creating any unlawful restraints on competition or the appearance of any unlawful restraints.

In the United States, certain types of agreements with third parties, including competitors, suppliers, or customers are unlawful *per se* under federal antitrust law. That is, such agreements are automatically in violation of such laws, regardless of the agreements, commercial reasonableness, its purpose, or its actual effect on competition. Other agreements with competitors or customers, although not unlawful *per se*, may be unlawful under the antitrust "rule of reason."

Formal or informal arrangements with actual or potential competitors (a broadly defined group) which limit or restrict competition may constitute *per se* violations. Such unlawful agreements include those which: fix, stabilize, or control prices (also a broadly defined term which includes not only price but any element of price such as credit terms, discounts, freight rates, etc.) or terms or conditions of sale; allocate products, markets, customers, or territories; boycott customers or suppliers; or limit or prohibit a party from carrying on a particular commercial enterprise. To assure compliance with antitrust laws, Company employees are not to enter into any discussion or arrangements with an actual or potential competitor which could result in any such *per se* violation. Further, since the existence of an unlawful agreement may be inferred from the mere exchange of competitively sensitive information between competitors, absent prior review and approval by Company counsel that such actions are lawful no employee shall give to or accept from a competitor any information concerning prices, terms, and conditions of sale, or any other competitive information.

Certain types of restrictive understandings between a customer and supplier are also deemed to be anti-competitive and may be *per se* antitrust violations. Some such agreements are clearly *per se* illegal, such as an agreement between a supplier and a distributor setting the distributor's minimum resale prices. Others may be *per se* illegal if the party imposing the agreement has market power, such as an agreement imposing a required of reciprocal dealing, (for example, an agreement that one party buys goods from another only or the understanding that the second party will buy goods from the first), or tying a customer's right to buy one product or service to the obligation to buy another. These possible *per se* illegal arrangements must not be agreed to or discussed with a customer, absent prior review and approval by Company counsel that the arrangement is lawful.

Agreements that do not unambiguously injure competition (*i.e.,* that are not *per se* illegal) are analyzed under the antitrust rule of reason. Under the antitrust "rule of reason" test, a court determines whether a particular agreement acts as an "unreasonable" restraint on trade and thus is anti-competitive and unlawful. Such a determination is based on a particular set of facts and circumstances, including the terms of the agreement, the purposes, the relationship of the parties, and the probable effects on competition. Since the circumstances surrounding any arrangement change from time to time, it is essential that agreements which could potentially cause an unreasonable restraint on trade be subject to continuing review by Company legal counsel.

Unilateral action by the Company (in other words, conduct not involving an agreement) may also violate the antitrust laws. Any transaction or practice that would appear to result in the Company gaining a monopoly in a particular line of business in a particular market or geographic area, or which indicates an intent to drive a competitor out of business or to prevent a competitor from entering a market, should therefore be avoided and discussed with Company legal counsel.

Also, discriminating pricing can violate a complicated antitrust statute known as the Robinson-Patman Act.

The sanctions resulting from violations of the antitrust laws can be severe, both as to corporations and as to individuals; they include both criminal penalties and civil treble damages. Whenever any question arises as to the significance or application of antitrust laws, Company legal counsel must be consulted, and any agreements with possible antitrust implications shall be made only with prior approval of Company legal counsel.

International operations may be subject to antitrust laws of either the United States or foreign countries, so employees should be aware of the implication of any such laws to Company transactions.

Advice should be sought in respect of equivalent requirements under other applicable jurisdictions, including the European Commission.

COMPLIANCE WITH ENVIRONMENTAL LAWS

Employees of Enron Corp., its subsidiaries, and its affiliated companies (collectively the "Company") must conduct Company operations in compliance with all applicable environmental laws and regulations including those of other countries which have jurisdiction over Company activities. These laws are designed to protect the environment in which we live and work, human health, wildlife, and natural resources. Environmental laws either prohibit or severely restrict the release of pollutants to the air, land, surface water, and groundwater. They contain numerous waste management requirements. They impose on owners and operators of most types of facilities the duty to protect the environment by requiring them to obtain permits for certain emissions, to report release and spills of materials which may cause pollution, and to create and maintain certain records. The Company is committed to environmental protection, and it expects employees to abide by the letter and the spirit of these laws. Employees who do not follow environmental rules and regulations shall be subject to appropriate disciplinary action.

Those responsible for the construction and the operation of Company facilities must ensure that the Company has the necessary environmental permits and clearances for these activities and that the Company complies with the terms and conditions of its permits. These individuals are charged with the responsibility of ensuring that the Company makes all required environmental reports and maintains, at the appropriate location, all required environmental records. Employees must consider the environmental consequences of all aspects of Company operations and proposed changes to our operations.

One of the major environmental laws of the United States may have significant legal and economic consequences for companies which fail to consider the environmental aspects of proposes transactions. The Comprehensive Environmental Response, Compensation and Liability Act (CERCLA, commonly known as "Superfund") was passed to provide a means for cleaning up abandoned waste disposal sites and for responding to environmental emergencies. CERCLA imposes sweeping liability (i) on those who sent hazardous substances to sites that may be cleaned up under CERCLA, (ii) on those who owned or operated these sites when hazardous substances were sent there, (iii) on those who transported hazardous substances to these sites, and (iv) on those who now own or operate these sites. These four classes of persons are potentially responsible for the entire cost of cleaning up the site. Employees must attempt to avoid actions which would increase the Company's Superfund liability. Those who are responsible for disposing waste offsite should ensure that the disposal facility is well managed by a reputable firm. Those who engage in real estate transactions of any nature, particularly acquiring property rights, should make all appropriate inquiry about environmental conditions at the property before completing the real estate transaction.

Environmental regulations change constantly both in the United States and abroad. These who are responsible for environmental compliance should make every effort to stay abreast of changes to regulations which affect the Company and to plan accordingly for the implementation of regulations which have been proposed.

Environmental audits may be used to verify compliance with environmental regulations. The U.S. Environmental Protection Agency and the Department of Justice encourage the performance of periodic, internal environmental audits to ensure compliance with regulatory requirements. The Company likewise encourages those in charge of operations to conduct periodic environmental audits of Company facilities.

The Company encourages the efforts of employees to minimize the quantity of waste generated by Company operations and to recycle waste which is produced. Innovative waste minimization not only protects the environment by reducing the volume of waste generated, it may also result in reduced operating costs for the Company.

All employees should be aware that the violation of environmental laws may result in the imposition of significant civil and criminal penalties for the Company as well as for individual employees. Many of the laws that apply to the Company's operations in the U.S. provide for civil penalties in the amount of $25,000 per violation, and they make each day of violation a separate offense. Criminal penalties for environmental violations may be as much as fifteen (15) years imprisonment per violation. Severe criminal and civil penalties for environmental violations may also be imposed in other countries in which the Company conducts its business.

Advice should be sought with respect to requirements and powers of enforcement agencies in jurisdictions outside of the United States.

CONFLICTS OF INTERESTS, INVESTMENTS AND
OUTSIDE BUSINESS INTERESTS OF OFFICERS AND EMPLOYEES

Employees of the Company have inquired from time to time as to the propriety of their association with, or the investment of their personal funds in, business enterprises similar in character to certain activities of the Company. In response, the Company has established certain principles for the guidance of officers and employees with respect to personal business and investment interests.

The primary consideration of each full-time (regular as well as temporary) officer and employee should be the fact that the employer is entitled to expect of such person complete loyalty to the best interests of the Company and the maximum application of skill, talent, education, etc., to the discharge of his or her job responsibilities, without any reservations. Therefore, it follows that no full-time officer or employee should:

(a)   Engage in any outside activity or enterprise which could interfere in any way with job performance;

(b)   Make investments or perform services for his or her own or related interest in any enterprise under any circumstances where, by reason of the nature of the business conducted by such enterprise, there is, or could be, a disparity or conflict of interest between the office or employee and the Company; or

(c)   Own an interest in or participate, directly or indirectly, in the profits of any other entity which does business with or is a competitor of the Company, unless such ownership or participation has been previously disclosed in writing to the Chairman of the Board and Chief Executive Officer of Enron Corp. and such officer has determined that such interest or participation does not adversely affect the best interests of the Company.

Notwithstanding any provision to the contrary in this Policy on Investments, securities of publicly-owned corporations which are regularly traded on the open market may be owned without disclosure if they are not purchased as a result of confidential knowledge about the Company's operations, relations, business, or negotiations with such corporations.

If an investment of personal funds by an officer or employee in a venture or enterprise will not entail personal services or managerial attention, and if there appears to be no conflict or disparity of interest involved, the following procedure nevertheless shall be followed if all or any part of the business of the venture or enterprise is identical with, or similar or directly related to, that conducted by the Company, or if such business consists of the furnishing of goods or services of a type utilized to a material extent by the Company:

(a)   The officer or employee desiring to make such investment shall submit in writing to the Chairman of the Board and Chief Executive Officer of Enron Corp. a brief summary of relevant facts; and

(b)   The Chairman of the Board and Chief Executive Officer of Enron Corp. shall consider carefully the summary of relevant facts, and if he concludes that there appears to be no probability of any conflict of interest arising out of the proposed investment, the officer or employee shall be so notified and may then make the proposed investment in full reliance upon the findings of the Chairman of the Board and Chief Executive Officer of Enron Corp.

148

In the event the Chairman of the Board and Chief Executive Officer of Enron Corp. should desire to make such an investment, he may do so only upon approval of the majority of a quorum of the Executive Committee of the Board of Directors of Enron Corp., other than himself, at any regular or special meeting of such Committee.

Every officer and employee shall be under a continuing duty to report, in the manner set forth above, any situation where by reason of economic or other interest in an enterprise there is then present the possibility of a conflict or disparity of interest between the officer or employee and the Company. This obligation includes but is not limited to (1) any existing personal investment at the date of promulgation of this policy, (2) any existing personal investment at the time of employment of any officer or employee by the Company, and (3) any existing personal investment, whether or not previously approved, which may become in conflict with the provisions of this policy because of changes in the business of the Company or changes in the business of the outside enterprise in which investment has been made.

In the event of a finding by the Chairman of the Board and Chief Executive Officer of Enron Corp. (or by the Executive Committee of the Board of Directors of Enron Corp., if applicable) that a material conflict or disparity of interest does exist with respect to any existing personal investment of an officer or employee, then, upon being so notified, the officer or employee involved shall immediately divest himself or herself of such interest and shall notify the Chairman and Chief Executive Officer of Enron Corp. (or the Executive Committee, if applicable) in writing that he or she has done so.

RESPONSIBILITY FOR REPORTING

The Company has established a reporting systems that allows officers, employees, and other agents of the Company to report violations of any of the Policies set forth in this booklet, or other Company policies, as well as any suspected criminal conduct by any officer, employee, or agent of the Company relating to the performance of his or her duties.

Upon observing or learning of any such violation or criminal conduct employees should report the same by writing a letter describing the suspected violation or criminal conduct with as much detail as possible and sending the letter to:

> Enron Compliance Officer
> CONFIDENTIAL – Conduct of Business Affairs
> P.O. Box 1188
> Houston, Texas 77251-1188

Employees may also report the same by telephoning the Office of the Chairman of the Company at (713) 853-7294 or sending an e-mail addressed to the Office of the Chairman. If an employee places the call from his or her extension, or an outside line, the message will be completely anonymous. Similarly, e-mail addressed to the Officer of the Chairman will also be completely anonymous.

The employee may (but is not required to) sign the letter or e-mail. Anonymous letters and anonymous e-mail will be investigated and acted upon in the same manner as letters and e-mail which contain a signature. All letters and e-mail should contain as much specific detail as possible to allow the Company to conduct an investigation of the reported matter.

All letters, e-mail and telephone calls submitted shall be kept in confidence and acted upon only by designated objective Company personnel unless disclosure is required or deemed advisable in connection with any governmental investigation or report, in the interest of the Company, or in the Company's legal handling of the matter. The Company will not condone any form of retribution upon any employee who uses the reporting system in good faith to report suspected wrongdoers, unless the individual reporting is one of the violators. The Company will not tolerate any harassment or intimidation of any employee using the reporting system.

COMPLIANCE, ADMINISTRATION

It is a condition of employment that each employee accept the responsibility of complying with the foregoing policies. The Company will require each employee of the Company to complete and submit a statement in a form designated by the Company pertaining to such employee's compliance with the policies set forth in this booklet. The Company reserves the right to request any employee to complete and submit such statement at any time or as frequently as the Company may deem advisable.

The Chairman of the Board and Chief Executive Officer of Enron Corp. may from time to time at the Chairman's discretion delegate any of the responsibilities to be fulfilled by the Chairman as hereinabove set forth. Such delegation may be made to any executive officer of the Company.

An employee who violates any of these policies is subject to disciplinary action including but not limited to suspension or termination of employment, and such other action, including legal action, as the Company believes to be appropriate under the circumstances.

ACKNOWLEDGMENTS

I would like to express my thanks and sincere appreciation to my following colleagues and assistants at Foley & Lardner for their outstanding contributions and assistance in the creation of this book. Thank you!

Judy Peters

Pacha Grissom

Susie Christiansen

Donna Schultz

Cleta Mitchell

Jim McKeown

Larry Lynch

Martin Weinstein

Mary Sherwood

Laura Roberts

Jocelyn Brumbaugh

And, of course, a huge thanks to my wife, Cherie, and children, Dani and Robbie, for putting up with the many lost weekends and nights while Dad was writing this book.

BIBLIOGRAPHY

Business Ethics Policies. Chesterland, Ohio: Business Laws, Inc., 2002.

Creating and Maintaining an Ethical Corporate Climate. Washington, D.C.: Georgetown University Press, 1990.

Kile, Daniel A. *Business Conduct and Ethics: How to Set Up a Self-Governance Program.* Chesterland, Ohio: Business Laws, Inc., 1995.

Murphy, Patrick. *Eighty Exemplary Ethics Statements.* Notre Dame, IN: University of Notre Dame Press, 1998.

Seglin, Jeffrey L. *Do It Right.* MBA Jungle, November 2001.

ABOUT THE AUTHOR

Steven R. Barth is a partner in the Business Law Department of Foley & Lardner's Milwaukee office. As a member of the Transactional and Securities Practice Group, Mr. Barth practices in the areas of mergers, acquisitions, leveraged recapitalizations, and buyouts; venture capital and private equity fund formation and portfolio company investment; public and private offerings of equity and debt securities; public corporation securities laws and reporting compliance; corporate governance and ethics; and assisting in the organization, development, and financing of startup and development-stage corporations. Mr. Barth also specializes in counseling mid-market and closely held firms, including many family businesses. He has assisted many mid-sized companies in adopting and implementing their corporate codes of conduct and strategic plans and transitioning ownership and management to the next family generation, to employees, and to strategic or financial buyers.

Mr. Barth has represented buyers, sellers, investors, and intermediaries in more than 220 business combination transactions aggregating over $15.8 billion in total consideration. He has worked on deals both domestically and internationally, involving both publicly held and private corporations, over a broad range of industries. Mr. Barth also has represented issuers or underwriters in 40 public securities offerings raising over $4.1 billion. He currently represents four publicly traded companies, including Fresh Brands, Inc. (Piggly Wiggly and Dick's supermarkets), Northland Cranberries, Inc. (cranberry juice beverages), The Marcus Corporation (motels, hotels, and theaters), and Edison Control Corporation a/k/a Construction Forms, Inc. (manufacturer of industrial piping systems). Mr. Barth also is one of Robert W. Baird & Co., Inc.'s (regional investment banking firm) primary outside counsels.

Mr. Barth is a frequent speaker on acquisition issues, financing transactions, corporate ethics, SEC compliance, and corporate governance matters. He serves on the board of directors of Fresh Brands, Inc., the Milwaukee Economic Development Corporation (quasi-public agency that provides funding to developing companies), the Business Law Section of the Wisconsin State Bar, the Independent Business Association of Wisconsin (Wisconsin business owners association dedicated to political and economic enhancement), and several privately held growth companies.

Mr. Barth received his JD, *cum laude,* from the University of Michigan in 1984. He earned his BS, with highest distinction, in finance from Indiana University in 1981. While at Indiana University, he received the Elvis J. Stahr award as one of the University's top five graduating seniors. In 1997, Mr. Barth was selected by the *Milwaukee Business Journal* as one of Milwaukee's 40 leading professionals under 40 years of age.

BEST SELLING BOOKS

REFERENCE

Business Travel Bible – Must Have Phone Numbers, Business Resources & Maps
Business Grammar, Style & Usage – Rules for Articulate and Polished Business Writing and Speaking
ExecRecs – Executive Recommendations For The Best Products, Services & Intelligence Executives Use to Excel
The C-Level Test – Business IQ & Personality Test for Professionals of All Levels
The Business Translator-Business Words, Phrases & Customs in Over 65 Languages

MANAGEMENT/CONSULTING

Corporate Ethics – The Business Code of Conduct for Ethical Employees
Leading CEOs – CEOs Reveal the Secrets to Leadership & Profiting in Any Economy
Leading Consultants – Industry Leaders Share Their Knowledge on the Art of Consulting
Managing & Profiting in a Down Economy – Leading CEOs Reveal the Secrets to Increased Profits and Success in a Turbulent Economy
The Governance Game – Restoring Boardroom Excellence & Credibility in America
Leading Women – What It Takes to Succeed & Have It All in the 21st Century
Leading Deal Makers – Leveraging Your Position and the Art of Deal Making
The Art of Deal Making – The Secrets to the Deal Making Process
WhatIf Brainstormers – Question Blocks & Idea Worksheets
Management Brainstormers – Question Blocks & Idea Worksheets

TECHNOLOGY

Leading CTOs – The Secrets to the Art, Science & Future of Technology
Software Product Management – Managing Software Development from Idea to Development to Marketing to Sales
The Telecommunications Industry – Leading CEOs Share Their Knowledge on The Future of the Telecommunications Industry
Know What the CTO Knows – The Tricks of the Trade and Ways for Anyone to Understand the Language of the Techies
Web 2.0 AC (After Crash) – The Resurgence of the Internet and Technology Economy
The Semiconductor Industry – Leading CEOs Share Their Knowledge on the Future of Semiconductors
Technology Brainstormers – Question Blocks & Idea Development Worksheets

VENTURE CAPITAL/ENTREPRENEURIAL

Term Sheets & Valuations – A Detailed Look at the Intricacies of Term Sheets & Valuations Deal Terms – The Finer Points of Deal Structures, Valuations, Term Sheets, Stock Options and Getting Deals Done
Leading Deal Makers – Leveraging Your Position and the Art of Deal Making
The Art of Deal Making – The Secrets to the Deal Making Process
Hunting Venture Capital – Understanding the VC Process and Capturing an Investment
Entrepreneurial Momentum – Gaining Traction for Businesses of All Sizes to Take the Step to the Next Level
The Entrepreneurial Problem Solver – Entrepreneurial Strategies for Identifying Opportunities in the Marketplace
Entrepreneurial Brainstormers – Question Blocks & Idea Development Worksheets
Leading CEOs – CEOs Reveal the Secrets to Leadership & Profiting in Any Economy

To Order or For Customized Suggestions From an Aspatore Business Editor, Please Call 1-866-Aspatore (277-2867) Or Visit www.Aspatore.com

LEGAL

FINANCIAL

MARKETING/ADVERTISING/PR

OTHER

ASPATORE
C-Level Business Intelligence™